The
Glamour
Book

The Glamour Book

Edited by Robert Scott

BFP BOOKS London

© 1982 BFP Books
All rights reserved. No part of this publication may be reproduced, stored in a
retrieval system or transmitted in any form or by any means, without the written
permission of the publishers.
Every care has been taken in the compilation of this book, but the publishers can
assume no responsibility for any errors or omissions, or any effects arising
therefrom.

First edition 1982

ISBN 0 907297 01 3

Published by BFP Books, a division of the Bureau of Freelance Photographers,
Focus House, 497 Green Lanes, London N13 4BP, and printed in Great Britain by
A. Wheaton & Co. Ltd., Exeter.

Designed by Michael English Design Associates Ltd, Sheffield.
Typesetting by Typestyle, Chesterfield

Contents

Introduction

So you want to be a glamour photographer?

If you are thinking of becoming a glamour photographer, here is a word of advice. Don't.

If you are reading this next sentence, then you have one of the qualities needed to be a glamour photographer. Perserverance. Glamour photography looks like fun – pretty girls, sun-soaked beaches and a life with the jet-set.

It is not like that.

This book takes a look at six photographers who shoot glamour. All six take most of their pictures at home, or close by. Assignments abroad happen, but not often, and they are usually self-financed.

None of the six earns a living entirely from glamour photography. All work in other areas as well.

Despite this, there is no sign that any of them is ready to turn to anything else. There is a glamour surrounding glamour photography. There is a certain pleasure in making girls look beautiful in pictures, and there is a certain satisfaction in seeing these pictures in print.

The six photographers have been chosen because the style of their photography is simple and straightforward. Their indoor sets are inexpensive, their outdoor locations are local. They do not have assistants. Much of the glamour work they produce is speculative.

In short, any competent amateur photographer starts off with the same opportunities!

This book will not teach you how to take pictures. There are many other books available if you need to improve your photographic techniques.

Here, you will discover how other photographers approach glamour photography, and see some of the results they produce. You will be able to profit from their success – and learn from their mistakes!

Among the other pages, you will hear from the people who want to buy your photographs, and the girls you want to photograph. At the end are pages of useful addresses and telephone numbers.

This book cannot do all the work for you, though. If you want to be a successful glamour photographer – either in your spare time, or full-time – you must look forward to a lot of research, seeking out new markets for your pictures. Only about 20% of your time will be spent actually taking the shots. The other 80% will be tied up with sorting and selling.

But your first published picture will make it all worthwhile.

Most of the chapters in this book are based on interviews with photographers, editors and models. Most of these interviews were with Robert Scott; the Kenneth Bound interview was with Mike Gerrard. The six photographers and Robert Scott provided all the pictures.

We are grateful to everyone concerned for the time and trouble they took in helping to prepare this material.

Six
photographers

John Berry
Nigel Holmes
Ken Howard
Tom Hustler
Harvey Nielson
Colin Ramsay

John Berry's background is not that of a typical professional photographer. For a short period, he was driving buses around Birmingham, before joining a photographic importer as a sales representative.

During this time, he became more and more attracted to glamour photography, and had some success in selling his work. Finally, he decided to pursue a full-time career in professional photography, accepting commercial and industrial work in addition to weddings, portraits and glamour.

For a while, he ran a photographic studio and model agency at Cradley Heath, near Birmingham. However, he sold this business after finding that more and more of his time was taken up with administration.

Having to earn a living from photography meant that the glamour side suffered for quite a while. However, now that he is becoming more established, John Berry is finding a little time to pursue a few new ideas.

I started taking photographs when I was about seven or eight – of the girl next door! She was my heart-throb at the time.

I was taking photographs until I was about eighteen, and I wanted to become a professional photographer. So my father took me along to see one.

I now know that this photographer was not very good, but in those days his word was gospel. I showed him a few of my prints and he spent about half-an-hour telling me how good he was, and how wonderful it was to be a professional photographer – and that I would do better to forget about it. He put me off. I did not take another photograph for about ten years.

But then I fell in love with photography again. Gradually, it became more and more of a passion. I started to want awards and distinctions just for the sheer satisfaction of getting them.

At that time, I was photographing anything and everything that moved. But I have always liked women, so it was natural that I should start to photograph them.

I had taken various pictures of girl friends without much success, and then I went to a glamour weekend run by a photographic magazine. That did it for me. I started doing more and more photographs of girls – actually going out looking for models and hiring studios.

At that time, I had just started as a sales representative for a photographic company, and I carried on taking photographs.

Gradually, I started to build up a group of my own models – girls who I had introduced to modelling, or who now did a lot of work for me.

I was not selling many photographs at the time – just the odd ones here and there for greetings cards and calendars, and not always glamour.

In the meantime, I was having an argument with my employers, who wanted me to move to a position which would give less money. In the end, we parted company.

I had earned my Associateship of the Royal Photographic Society by then, and was aiming to become a full-time photographer eventually. But I really wanted a bit more behind me first. I had only been married about fifteen months, and we had just started to buy a house.

But needs must – so I got on to the bank manager and he agreed to back me.

I freelanced for a few months, submitting work to publishers as before, but with more determination. This gave better results. I earned about £700 in the first five months.

Then I set up my own business and the glamour side started to go by the board – I just did not have enough time. I had to find work which was more commercial. Very few people earn a living from glamour photography. Most have to do commercial work they don't like.

And I wanted a studio of my own. I was tired of hiring and taking along a background roll because they did not have one. Or using my lighting to supplement theirs. I managed, but it was difficult.

Eventually, I found a place. I spent six weeks knocking down walls, drying it out and decorating. And then it was ready.

Building the agency

I had a nucleus of about half-a-dozen girls I could call on once the studio was under way. However, I wanted to hire the studio out when I wasn't using it myself, so I needed a larger model directory. I decided that the best way to handle this was by opening a proper model agency.

Most studios that are available for amateur photographers tend to have models to match. And most model agencies that are used by professional photographers have a professional fee structure. I tried to aim down the middle, with good models for commercial photography, but friendly and accessible to amateurs.

When the agency started, I just advertised for girls locally, not knowing what response to expect.

It was unbelievable! For nearly six weeks, I did very little commercial work. I spent all my time interviewing girls.

The majority, of course, were useless, but there were a few inexperienced girls who looked promising. There was also a number of girls who had trained as models, but were not working full-time and wanted to come on the books.

We took twenty-five girls initially and ran model training courses for those who needed them. Some well-established models heard about the agency and came along to see us, including a lot of the local beauty queens.

There was a steady turnover, in fact, because some of the girls disappeared. They found a new boyfriend, who did not approve of modelling, or took a full-time job which left them less time – or they went abroad to work. One girl moved to Florida, another emigrated to Johannesburg, and a third left for Italy.

Because we aimed at a wider range of photographers than most agencies, we also offered a wide range of models. The youngest was 16, while the oldest was about 45 years. And it is amazing how many of the older girls were booked regularly by the older photographers – and even by the younger ones. It is not always the teenage models who get the work. A lot of photographers like girls in their thirties.

Our oldest model only did commercial and fashion work, but we had a woman in her late thirties who was booked for glamour work.

Model management

Talk to her. I think that is the most important advice I can give to anyone photographing a model. Bring her out. Make her feel at ease.

Nothing will give you worse pictures than a model who feels that she is being used like a lump of lead. Do not photograph her as if she is an inanimate object. She is not. She is a living person. She has a personality. She has interests and hobbies; things she likes and things she does not like. And she enjoys talking.

If the atmosphere is light and lively, you will get animated pictures. If it is tense, you will not.

Try to work quickly with a model – it will warm her up. It is much more difficult working slowly shot by shot, because there is no flow to the session. Without flow, the model will become static and tense.

Commercially, this can be a big problem. The brief will force you to work to a set format where it is not possible to shoot quickly. This makes it much more difficult to get the right atmosphere and expressions coming over in the photographs.

An amateur, or a freelance shooting to gain a little experience, can afford to waste a little film. It is worth wasting film to keep the model working – to keep her in the mood.

For people learning about glamour photography, I do not think there is any substitute for using film. It is the best way to see your mistakes – and to see the model.

Beginners are also going to obtain much better results if they start by using an experienced model – one they do not have to keep posing every few moments.

Then, when the photographer is more experienced, he can help a new model to improve.

A good basic lighting set-up for beginners is with just two lights, at about 45° on either side of the camera. In the studio, I use electronic flash with an umbrella reflector on one light and a diffuser on the other.

This suits most models. The illumination is soft and even, so you do not have to worry too much about how the girl is posing – there will be no awkward shadows. She can turn in most directions and the lighting will still be flattering.

With powerful studio flash, the photographer will be able to work with a lens aperture of f/11 or f/16 – giving plenty of depth-of-field. This is useful, because many photographers do not seem able to focus accurately when they start to work in a studio. They do not focus on the eyes, and so the results are terrible. With plenty of depth-of-field, there is more chance of acceptably sharp photographs!

If a third light is used, it usually goes behind or above the girl to light the hair. Two more lights can be used to give even background illumination.

That is a lot of light, but a good studio will be able to provide it. But even with all these lights, the basic set-up is still very simple.

I think two hours is the shortest period for which it is worth booking a studio.

A lot of photographers book for an hour, and then find they are only just getting into the swing of things when the time is up. Bookings, of course, are inclusive from the moment of

Work quickly with your model, especially if she is inexperienced. If you stop to change the lighting or alter the pose after every shot, she will become tense. Instead, expose a dozen frames within the first few minutes of the photo session, so that the girl gains confidence and relaxes. Of course, not all of these pictures will be successful. Some of the expressions will be poor. The poses will not be perfect. But you will often find one or two photographs which are quite acceptable from this first film.

walking into the studio before the session, to the final moment of cleaning up at the end. Somebody else may be waiting to use the studio immediately after.

If the photographer has worked with the same model before, and built a rapport, then perhaps they can get quite a lot of work done in an hour. But most people usually need two hours.

If special studio set-ups are needed, then it can sometimes be worthwhile for the photographer to book the studio a quarter-of-an-hour, or even half-an-hour in advance of the model. For straightforward pictures, though, there is no real need. The studio can be set up while the model is changing.

How many photographs can be taken in a couple of hours? How long is a piece of string?

We had one client who came over from Holland every two or three months. He was a

Many ideas for photographs can be found by looking through glamour calendars. These often feature girls in water. You may not be able to catch a plane to the Caribbean for your next photo session, but you can shoot at a swimming pool. A public swimming pool, though, is not the ideal place to take glamour pictures. Instead, find a hotel with a pool and talk to the Conference Manager. You will find that it is often possible to use the pool at a quiet time of day for less than the cost of hiring a studio.

very serious photographer, and very experienced with glamour. He booked the studio for two hours, though he rarely worked that long. But he studied very closely every photograph he took. I have known him shoot as few as twelve pictures in one session!

On the other hand, some photographers will happily run through half-a-dozen films in an hour. You just cannot say.

People working with 35mm, though, tend to shoot a lot more than roll-film users. In a two-hour session, photographers with a medium-format camera will probably get through eight or nine 12-exposure films. But there are a lot of 35mm users who will shoot nine or ten 36-exposure cassettes in the same period.

Hiring a model

I operated a two-tier fee system for booking a model – commercial and non-commercial.

The non-commercial rate enabled photographers to submit their work to photographic magazines and photographic competitions, or use them in club competitions, but that is all. There was no model release supplied.

If photographers needed a model release from the girl, they had to book at the commercial rate. This covered most commercial uses. But a separate fee had to be negotiated if the photographs were for calendars, men's magazines or national advertising.

This is only fair to the girls. If their photographs are used in a major advertising campaign, they deserve more money than if the pictures only appear at camera club competitions.

The system also gave us more control over the photographs taken. The model knew beforehand the type of photographs she was expected to pose for, and did not, for example, end up topless when she was only being paid for portraits.

The photographers also benefited. They knew whether or not a signed model release would be available at the end of the session. There was no argument about the girl not being paid until the release form was signed.

If an amateur photographer booked a girl at the non-commercial rate, and then found the photographs were good enough to sell, we would supply a model release for the difference between the non-commercial and commercial rates.

Some amateur photographers, unfortunately, are over-confident about their abilities. They book a girl at the commercial rate, hoping to make immediate sales. It is not until the films are processed that they realise their photography is not up to the required standard.

The main problem is a total lack of animation in the pictures.

The photographer has not brought out the personality of the model. There is no rapport between the camera and the girl.

Improving your pictures

A photographer who has not done much glamour work may find a short practical course quite useful.

The problem with many courses is that there are too many photographers taking photographs of too few models. And there will always be one or two people who dominate the sessions, setting the lighting and posing the girls.

But a lot can be learnt from watching other photographers at work, and seeing the mistakes they make. You may also come across new techniques which will work well for you.

Experienced photographers will gain more from seminars. These offer an exchange of ideas between professional photographers. There is a lot that can be learnt by listening to other people talking about the way they work, and how they overcome problems.

Many of the problems in photography are the same for everyone, so it is always useful to discover how other people have solved them.

Various types of photographic courses are run by the professional photographic organisations, some photographic studios, and a few of the photographic magazines. It is simply a matter of reading advertisements and writing off for details of any courses which seem interesting.

The experienced glamour photographer, though, is probably better off working on his own. He needs to come up with new ideas and then follow these up in the studio.

I look through all the photographic magazines to keep up with the latest trends. I frequently disagree with the ideas and photographs that are in these magazines, but at least they set me thinking.

Of course, some of the photographic techniques are outside the scope of the average photographer. They require giant studios, or large amounts of lighting equipment. There is no way that the same effects can be created with three flash units in a small room.

However, you can often adapt the basic idea to suit your own resources. The results will be different, but may be just as effective.

A lot of ideas for glamour poses can be found by looking at advertising photographs, and some of the better calendars. You just need to learn to look around. There is no such thing as an original idea. Every photographer takes ideas from other photographers.

Some of the quality men's magazines are well worth buying – they feature first-class photographs. Of course, it is a very specialised type of work, which is unlikely to sell elsewhere. Some of the ideas, though, can often be adapted to other types of photography.

Shooting to sell

You have to provide glamour magazines with what they want. There is a lot more to it than simply taking photographs of a nude girl. In some cases, it means shooting the pictures to suit the style of a particular magazine.

This is one of the problems of glamour photography. Your own likes and dislikes are not important. It is the picture editor you have to please. Since you may not know the picture editor, this can be difficult.

All you can do is study recent magazines and then go out and shoot similar photographs of similar girls – just different enough to have fresh appeal.

Of course, this still does not mean you will sell. The editor might have accepted a portfolio of pictures just like your new shots a few days earlier. If a magazine is not in the market for your particular pictures at that particular time, they will come back, no matter how good they are.

The other approach is to shoot the photographs you like, and then try to find a magazine which appreciates your style.

I have noticed that several of my models seem to work well together, and so I am working on some ideas for duo sets – not pornographic, but nice soft-focus glamour portfolios. I think there will be a good market for these, because there are fewer photographers shooting them.

You have to be very careful how you choose girls for this type of work. They not only have to be compatible and look good together, they also have to project the same mood at the same time.

Glamour photography is easier when you are shooting for a client. The client will help you select the model and brief you on the exact requirements for the photographs.

Most glamour sales, though, are speculative, and few professional photographers have the time to do proper research before shooting a new series of pictures.

This is where the amateur photographer can find an opening. The amateur does have the time.

Going it alone

I was out of work for a few months before I finally set up as a full-time professional photographer. This meant that I had a lot of time to spare. I used some of it going through my existing stock of glamour photographs and matching them up to the requirements listed in the monthly newsletters from the Bureau of Freelance Photographers.

I made quite a lot of money out of this. It was not a living wage, but it was a very reasonable return for the amount of time and effort expended.

But the moment you turn professional, the situation changes. It becomes much more difficult to justify the time spent in this sort of activity.

The amateur who is doing quite nicely as a part-time freelance glamour photographer needs to think very carefully before turning professional.

The majority would be very foolish to give up a well-paid full-time job and a useful extra income from photography in the hope of earning a living from full-time glamour photography.

It is more than likely that they would find themselves being paid very small fees for photography which did not interest them. As a professional, you have to shoot what the client wants, whether you like it or not.

This is the real difference between an amateur and a professional, and it is why my own personal photography has gone by the board during the last couple of years. I just have not had the time to take pictures for myself.

Camera choice

For somebody starting glamour photography, 35mm is the best format.

First, equipment is a lot cheaper in the smaller format. Second, it is easier to handle in the studio. Third, a 35mm single-lens reflex camera system offers a good range of interchangeable lenses at a reasonable price.

It is useful to have a variety of lenses so that you can always work at a comfortable distance from the model, whether you are taking a head-shot, or a full-length photograph.

Occasionally, I use an 80-200mm zoom lens. This focuses fairly close, so that I can do anything from a close-up to a full-length with the one lens. It lets me compose the image more accurately in the camera. I can crop the picture without having to move the camera.

But although 35mm is good for a beginner, I do not think a more experienced photographer can do better than a medium-format camera.

I use a Bronica ETR. This is a roll-film single-lens reflex which gives the rectangular 6 x 4.5cm format. I like this. Having learnt about photography using 35mm cameras, I have become rectangular-minded. I find it very difficult to use a 6 x 6cm format camera, because I don't think square.

Also, if you are shooting in a studio, it is very difficult to avoid lighting stands or the edges of a background on the sides of a square format film. This does not matter if you are shooting negative film, because a print can be made from just the central area of the frame, but it can be a problem with transparency film.

With a 6 x 4.5cm format, you can crop the image in the camera.

I do not like using tripods in a studio. I find them restrictive. I find them static. You never get any variation in your shots. The Bronica is not too heavy. It is a nicely-balanced camera which I can hold in my hand.

Unfortunately, not all processing laboratories can print from the 6 x 4.5cm format, so you are restricted in your choice.

I use two laboratories. For normal work, there is a laboratory not far from my studio which is very good. They deal mainly with professionals, but handle work from some amateur photographers, as well.

If I need films processing fairly quickly, they will produce results in about three days, without any express surcharge.

My other laboratory takes longer, cannot be rushed, and is further away – but their processing is superb. Transparencies and colour prints are brilliant. However, I can only afford to use them for really critical work. It cuts down my profit if I have to take time off to drive over to the laboratory – not to mention the petrol costs.

I do not like using the postal service. I do not trust it. I have lost work in the post before. Even if you register a parcel, you worry about whether it will get there. They have a habit of losing things.

My advice is to find a small, local laboratory that will give a personal service. The problem with a lot of larger laboratories is that three-quarters of their work is very good, but you have to send the remaining quarter back for re-printing.

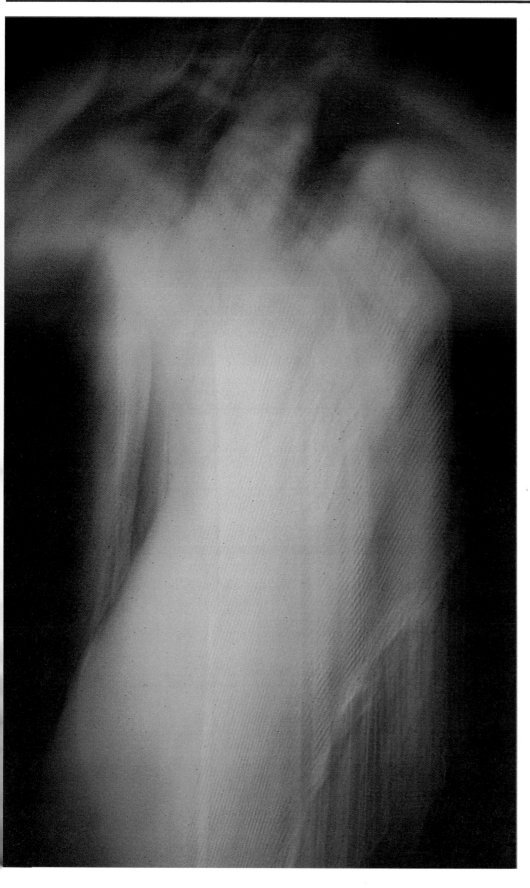

Here is a photograph which will not find its way into the pages of Mayfair magazine! But it is the sort of shot which could be used to illustrate creative techniques in a photographic magazine. Few professional photographers have the time to experiment with these effects, but time is the least expensive area for the amateur. Make a point of allowing time during your photo sessions for a few experimental techniques. You will encounter little competition in this small, but ready market.

Six photographers/Nigel Holmes

Bishop's Stortford, in Hertfordshire, would not be regarded by many as an ideal location for a glamour photographer. It is here, though, that Nigel Holmes is beginning to make a name for himself.

He started in a modest way, by selling pictures to photographic magazines while working in a High Street studio. Early success encouraged him to pursue glamour photography full-time, and he now works from his semi-detached home on one of the main roads out of town. The studio is also a lounge; the office is used by his wife as a workroom.

His bank balance was improved by the top prize of £3000 from a Men Only *nude photographic competition.*

I don't have any GCEs or CSEs. I am not qualified to do anything. So I became a photographer!

At school, I was pretty good at art. When I left, I went to work for the local council as a signwriter, serving a four-year apprenticeship. Then, after a spell with another signwriter, I went to EMI as a display artist/designer.

Next, I tried freelance design – just leaflet and local advertising. It was a disaster! But as a freelance, I came in contact with photographers and got to know the local High Street photographer quite well. Suddenly, he said, "do you want a job?" So I went to work for him.

I thought he was stupid. I did not know anything about photography. My camera was a Halina 35X which I used for holiday snaps.

I worked there for three years doing all the menial tasks, but he taught me one end of the camera from the other, and showed me how to process and print. And he taught me a lot of the basics – lighting, posing and how to control people.

I used to go to weddings with him, just carrying the case and loading films at first. He was – still is – a Fellow of the Institute of Incorporated Photographers and did not want to lose his reputation through me. But after a year, he let me go out on my own.

It was good experience. If there were 200 people at the wedding, he wanted a shot showing all 200. That meant you quickly learnt how to handle and control people.

Going for glamour

Then I started to photograph girls – I am not sure if it was by accident or not. I just drifted that way.

Perhaps it was because I was not allowed to take portraits of clients at the High Street studio. They were paying quite high fees and they obviously expected to be photographed by my employer, not by me.

The only way for me to get any portrait experience was by asking people if I could take their pictures, so I did. And it gradually drifted into glamour work.

I suppose I used to look at the glamour pictures in the photographic magazines and think, "I can do that." No doubt hundreds of other people think the same. But then I took what I thought was a really nice picture and decided to send it off to what was then *Camera User* magazine.

They wrote back and said they were interested and did I have any more photographs? I think they liked the pictures because they were different to the standard style of portraiture. My shots were not the usual blue blackground and brightly-lit model.

In the end, *Camera User* published a three-page feature on my work – not bad for my first submission, although I did not get much money from it.

But it made me think that there must be something more I could do, so I began to look at the photographic magazines a little more carefully. It soon became clear that there was a certain style of photograph which sold well. I shot a few rolls of film in this style – and *Amateur Photographer* used one of the pictures on their cover. Just like that!

I kept sending my work to various magazines and more of it was published. "Well," I thought, after a few months, "if I try a bit harder, I might be able to make a living out of this." So when another of my photographs was published on the cover of *Amateur Photographer,* I gave in my notice.

I had no regular income, no contracts, no retainers. I simply decided to stop working for someone else and start on my own.

Of course, I had worked freelance before, so I knew what was involved. The money coming in was cut in half, but if there is something you want to do, you must be prepared to take risks.

I do not regret my decision. It is working nicely now. I still have a long way to go, but people are beginning to know who I am.

Starting from scratch

As soon as I was on my own again, I went to the local library and searched through all the trade directories. I was looking for the people who might be interested in my work. Many were the local advertising agencies, who I had made contact with the last time I had been freelancing.

I went to see these people and said, "Look, it's me, I'm here. This is what I'm going to do. If you ever feel that you need what I do, then get in touch."

I try not to take on anything apart from glamour photography, but that is not always possible – there is still the mortgage to pay. So, within reason, I do anything I think I can handle.

For example, the first pictures I sold to *Practical Photography* were of a blue-tit feeding on a bag of peanuts in my garden, taken through double glazing.

I also sold *Homemaker* magazine a short article about a Christmas table decoration I made, with a series of black-and-white pictures showing the step-by-step construction.

And all this while, I have been building up a library of stock pictures.

The very first picture I sold was of a girl I met while working with the local hospital radio station. She used to do a lot of the broadcasting. My shots were taken at the High Street studio with her fully clothed.

After this, I used to find models by stopping girls in the street! I would go up to them and explain that I was a glamour photographer. Then I would ask if they had ever thought of being a model.

As soon as you say that, they think, "Who? Me?" And that is the time to give them a business card with your telephone number and walk away. It is no use pressing for an answer there and then. Give them time to think about it – and wait for the phone call.

For every ten girls that I approached, about eight would ring back – I was quite surprised. But then, I knew the type of girls I was looking for in the first place. I like to think that I can tell whether or not a girl will pose for pictures.

Of course, of those eight girls, only one or two were good enough to sell photographs.

To start with, I did not pay the girls anything. I simply agreed to pay them a percentage of any sales I made. This meant that the photographs only cost me the film. If I did not sell them, then I had not lost much.

But I soon found that I could not run a business this way. My profits were being given to the girl every time I sold more than two or three of her pictures. It is much better to pay the girl a single fee for the photo session, and then keep all the money you get from selling a lot of the pictures.

You might think this is a bit unfair on the girl, of course, but business is business.

It does mean, though, that you have to have confidence in your work. If you are paying the girl a reasonable fee, you cannot afford to shoot pictures which will not sell.

This is especially true now that I am using professional models from agencies.

Do photographs of professional models sell better than photographs of girls I have approached in the street? I am not sure. Almost all the pictures I take of one of my very first models seem to sell – it is very much a matter of finding the right girl.

But it is not such hard work photographing professional models. I use a couple of large model agencies and their girls really know what they are doing.

Surprisingly, though, it is not always easy to book top models.

The agency likes to know who you are first. Nobody wanted to know me at the start. Then I managed to find an agency that was willing to take a chance. Of course, once you have a few photographs of a girl from one agency, you can use these to persuade other agencies that you are genuine.

It might be worth trying your luck with a small agency to begin with. The only trouble is that they cannot offer the best girls. The best girls go to the bigger agencies. It is a Catch 22 situation.

Planning the sessions

I plan each of my glamour sessions very carefully. I like to know exactly what I am going to do before I start shooting.

For a few days beforehand, I will turn some ideas over in my mind, and then sit down and start sketching. My sketches are very basic, but they show what I want to do.

Each sketch has its own little square of paper. When I have put down all my ideas, I shuffle the squares together and spread them out face up in front of me.

I look for set-ups which will use similar lighting, or the same background, and put them together. Then I will see that the only difference between two ideas is, say, a change of coloured gel over the lights, so those sketches are placed next to each other. I end up with what should be the most sensible shooting sequence.

There is no point, for example, shooting one set-up on a black background, the next on red, and then changing back to black again. It takes time to move the backgrounds around. If you can sort out a sequence which lets you shoot all the black background pictures together, and then all the red background pictures, you will have time to take more pictures.

Mind you, when the transparencies come back, I jumble them all up so that no one sees that I have been shooting a lot of similar photographs!

When I am shooting, I also keep in mind the different types of market which might buy the pictures. This can mean that I shoot the same set-up three different ways.

For example, the girl might start off in a bikini for one type of market, then go topless and finally nude. The three sets of pictures can be taken very quickly, but give the chance of three different areas for selling.

A day's photo session will give me about 200 pictures. That's a comfortable number for me. I know that I can shoot about 20 different ideas in one day, so that is what I aim for.

It means that I take about ten different shots of each idea, and that includes the topless and nude alternatives.

Of course, you have to stay flexible. An idea will occur as you start to take the pictures, or you find that one of the set-ups will not work with the model you are using that day.

Some photographers seem to use a lot more film to obtain the results they want. I try to work out what I want before I start shooting.

The portrait photographer I used to work for is very much a one-shot man. He will take one picture and it will be right. And because that was the way I was trained, it is still the way I work.

Of course, I am not saying that I only need to take one shot – the model might blink! But I know in my mind what I want, and I only start shooting when I can see it in the camera.

I suppose part of this also comes from having worked with amateur models for so long. They never know what to do, so you have to lead all the time. This makes you very aware of exactly what is happening in front of the lens.

When you start planning your photo session, it can help to know the girl you will be photographing. A professional model will be able to adapt to most of your ideas, but is she blonde or brunette?

An amateur model may be much better at certain types of pictures than at others. You will only discover this after your first photo session with her.

Meeting the markets

How do I find new markets? With difficulty!

There is a large newsagent in town with hundreds of magazines on its shelves. I use it rather like a reference library! Whenever I go in, I have a small notepad and pencil in my pocket. If I see a shot in any magazine that I think I could have done, I make a note of the publisher's name and address. Later, I write to them asking if they would like to see any of my work. There are a lot of rejections, but occasionally it comes off.

Then there are all the mentions in the Bureau of Freelance Photographers' *Market Newsletter*. I found *Club Mirror* in there. I had no idea what sort of pictures they wanted, but sent a couple of shots anyway. The editor returned them as unsuitable, but enclosed a complimentary copy of the newspaper to show the type of photographs they published. I sent back a whole batch of new pictures, and he kept thirteen. That is over a year's supply if he uses one a month!

Recently, I saw a calendar hanging on a garage workshop wall and asked if I could

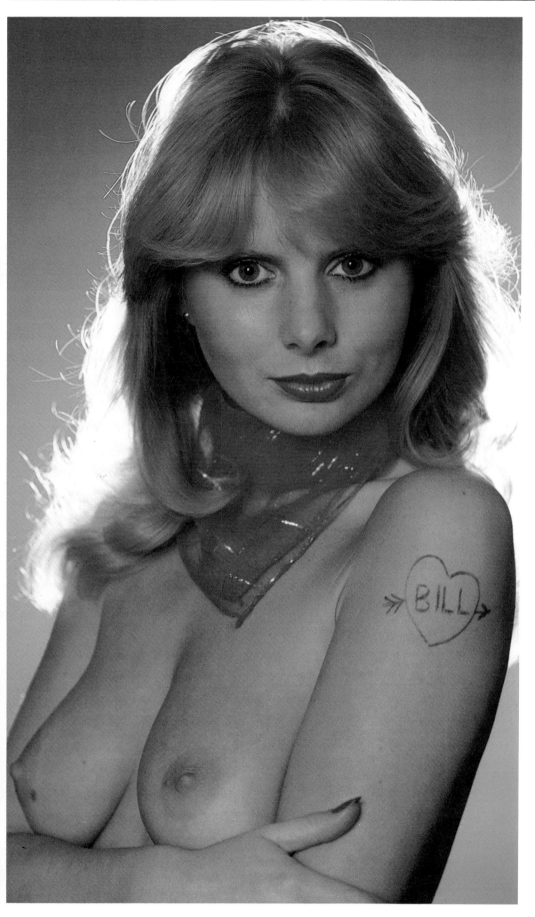

Carolyn Evans does not really have a boyfriend called Bill. This mark of affection on her arm is just a gimmick, drawn by the photographer. But it is a gimmick which worked. Within weeks of shooting, the photograph appeared in a national newspaper, complete with corny caption centred around the 'tattoo.' It is simple ideas like this which attract the attention of picture editors. Shoot half-a-dozen good ideas in a photo session and you will be well on the way to making photography pay.

Do not limit yourself to the clothes your model brings along to the photo session. Here, Gee is giving a new look to a shirt and tie from the photographer's wardrobe. Other male accessories worth trying include bow-ties, hats and caps, jackets and waistcoats. You will usually find that you get a completely different type of glamour shot from a girl as soon as she slips these clothes on.

have a look at it. They probably thought I was a dirty old man, but actually, I was taking down the name and address of the publisher. The publisher may give me the name and address of the picture agency which supplied the photographs, and they may be interested in seeing some of my work.

When I eventually find the contact I am looking for, I will send off a whole batch of photographs. Hopefully, a few will be retained – and then it's a matter of sitting back and waiting.

Calendar companies seem to work a couple of years ahead of everyone else. At the beginning of 1981, for example, I was sending out pictures for 1983 calendars. At the same time, some of the calendar shots I had sold two years earlier were just appearing.

I think my work has improved quite a lot in two years, because some of my published calendar pictures do not look too good to me now!

A new area for me at the moment is overseas sales. I was lucky here – an agent came across some of my work, liked it, and asked for more.

This is opening up new markets for my work. For some reason, photographs which I cannot sell in Britain will sell abroad. And overseas sales give new life to pictures which have already sold two or three times over here.

I still handle all the sales in Britain, and I have to be very careful to make sure similar pictures are not sent to different magazines in the same field. For example, I try not to send *Practical Photography* pictures from the same set of photographs submitted to *Amateur Photographer*. If I am dealing with one calendar company, I do not send them pictures similar to those which may be held by one of their competitors.

But you need to sell your photographs several times over if you have paid a top London model for a day's work. It is only when you pay lower rates to an amateur girl that you can hope to get by with single sales.

One of my photo sessions with a top model paid for itself after just three sales, and the photographs should keep on selling for several years. Against that, I have model sets which have only sold a single picture and are unlikely to make me a profit. Sometimes, you photograph a girl who just will not sell!

I would like to do more for glamour magazines, but it is a very difficult market. Each magazine seems to have a different policy. One likes pictures of the 'girl-next-door,' while another will only take photographs of girls with a model image. Some like to see the girls in glamorous settings, while others prefer simple backgrounds.

So if I photograph the 'girl-next-door' in a simple setting, there is only one magazine which is likely to be interested in the pictures. If they do not buy, there is little chance of selling elsewhere.

The only way you can win is by concentrating on a style for one magazine and submitting set after set of photographs until you succeed.

The trouble is, you never know whether it is your photography which is letting you down, or the girls.

The home studio

Nearly all my photographs are shot with a Bronica S2A – the camera I had when I started with wedding photography. I have two backs for the camera, so I can shoot black-and-white and colour without having to finish each film. And there is a 150mm lens in addition to the standard 75mm lens.

I am on my second tripod, the first was stolen from outside a church while I was photographing a wedding!

At first, I used the Bronica for everything, because I thought that all magazines preferred larger format transparencies. Then a few magazines sent my photographs back with a letter saying that they liked the style of my work, but preferred 35mm Kodachrome transparencies for reproduction.

I did not have a 35mm camera at the time, so I went out and bought a Minolta XG-2. I do not use it much, but the camera serves its purpose. I have sold photographs from it.

Originally, my lighting equipment consisted of two Courtenay Colourflash 2 studio

Of course it is corny, but a sexy six-shooter will sell! Do not race to copy this picture, though. You need to come up with your own corny ideas. You will not be able to afford all the accessories you need for each picture. See if you can come to some arrangement with a shop which hires out clothes for fancy dress parties. They are certain to have quiet times of the year when you can arrange special rates.

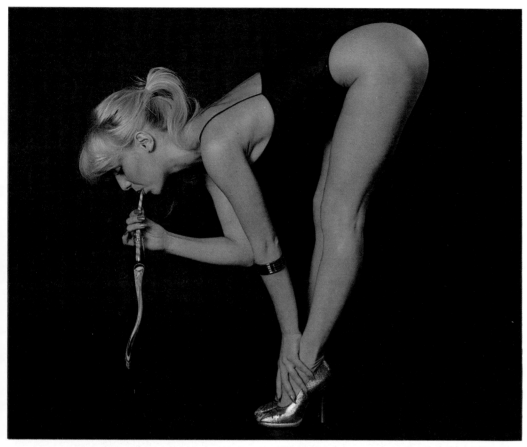

In any glamour set, different photographs should emphasise different features of the model. Here, it is the legs which attract attention. Only the slimmest girls will be able to produce this type of pose for you. But because it is unusual, this is a shot which will brighten up any portfolio of pictures.

Sporting themes are always popular for glamour photography. You only need the barest essentials to put over an idea. Keep all your shots simple. You are photographing a girl — everything else is secondary.

Opposite page
Some glamour pictures will only sell to limited markets because of the style of the shot. This photograph, for example, would not appeal to any newspapers, and it is unlikely to suit many magazines, but it could be just right for a calendar.

Compared with the picture opposite, this shot is much more saleable. Newspapers accepting topless pose would certainly consider it. And because there is nothing in the photograph which dates it, agencies and magazines with black-and-white glamour files would probably be happy to hold the picture for possible publication.

Seasonal glamour pictures are always in demand, especially at Christmas. If you look at the covers of magazines for December and January, you will see that many of the them feature a festive photograph. As with all glamour shots, the secret is to keep the set-up simple. Here, just a few brightly back-lit balloons are enough to tell you that the girl is in party mood.

flash units, which I bought before I gave up my studio job.

For the first year, all my work was done with these two lights, used with one large and one small gold umbrella. Fortunately, I had been trained to use a single light for portraiture at the portrait studio. There, two lights with umbrellas are placed side by side to create a single oval light source.

I also read that Peter Gowland, the American glamour photographer, tended to use a single light source with a huge reflector.

All my studio photography is done in my lounge at home. This room opens out to about 13 feet wide at one end, but is only 10 feet wide at the other. It is about 20 feet long.

I only had one roll of background paper – black. This was supported unsteadily by three pieces of timber. White backgrounds were taken against a cream-coloured wall!

I have gone up in the world now. I have two rolls of background paper, and I have added another flash unit – the Bowens 400. This has the advantage over the Courtenay units of variable power. I can alter the brightness of the flash without having to move the light.

My second background roll is grey, because grey seems to accept colours very well. If I want a coloured background, I just aim coloured light at the paper.

It used to take me quite a while to clear the lounge for photography, but now I can do it much quicker. I know where everything has to go, and how to turn the chairs a certain way to get them through the door.

I do some outdoor photography, but this has its limitations – mainly the British weather. I will go outside when I can, but this does not seem to be very often. I am waiting for a commission that will take me abroad!

Many people seem to think that a glamour photographer spends all his time in the studio. That is not what I have found. I use my home studio about once a week on average – although that can mean only once in some months, and six or seven times in others.

The rest of my time is spent writing letters, submitting transparencies to publishers, general administration, and filing.

I have a great filing system. Everyone I know is in my card index.

When I worked for EMI, I used to get sales representatives calling on me. They would walk in and say "Hello, Nigel, how's the wife?" And you would wonder how they managed to remember everything about you. In fact, they keep a filing system in their car where they can refresh their memory about each client before they call.

Well, I am a sales representative as well. My card index is close to the phone, so if a model rings, I can answer with the phone in my left hand while sorting out her card with my right. That reminds me who she is, the work she has done for me, the name of her boyfriend, and anything else I have picked up. I could not hope to remember everything otherwise.

Every transparency I shoot is also filed. I can tell you where every picture I own is sitting at this moment – whether it is in my files, or out with a publisher.

Each job I shoot has its own index card and file number. Each photograph from that job also has its own number. And the job number appears on the card of the model featured in the photographs.

Every time a transparency leaves me, I make a note of it. Every time one is returned, I make a note of it. I know who they have been sent to, who has used them, and who has rejected them.

But it is worth remembering that a rejection does not always mean that your work is not good enough. It may mean that the publisher cannot make use of it at that time. It is often worth re-submitting the same transparencies a year or so later. I have had photographs accepted like this the second time around!

An efficient filing system is very important, even though it sometimes seems that more time is spent on this than actually taking the pictures.

Out of London

So far, I have not come across any real problems from working as a glamour photographer outside London. If I have the photographs somebody wants, I can send them to him.

Settings for glamour photography need not be expensive. You can, quite literally, use a corner of a room for your pictures. In this shot, the wood panelling adds a touch of luxury without offering any distraction. Wood panelling can now be bought in large sheets, just right for leaning against brightly-flowered wallpaper!

The only disadvantage is with London models. I have to book them for a day, or half-day, and pay travelling expenses, too. If I was in London, I would only need to book them for a couple of hours at a time.

I have made sure my neighbours know what I do, because it might otherwise look a bit strange. For example, my wife goes to work at 9 am and I am alone in the house. Then a car drives up and a blonde gets out and I let her in. At 5pm, the blonde leaves and my wife returns at 6pm!

When people ask what I do for a living, I just say that I am a photographer. They assume that you mean passports and weddings, but if they keep asking questions, I explain that I am a glamour photographer.

The next question is always, "What does your wife think about it?"

People have a strange opinion of glamour photographers. I was chatting to an attractive girl at a party when somebody said jokingly to her husband, "I'd watch him if I were you – he takes photographs of ladies with their clothes off." Right away, the husband came and sat with us!

I would not advise other would-be glamour photographers to do what I have done – unless they are in a similar position. I had a job which did not seem to offer much for the future – and I have a very understanding wife! After all, there are not many wives who would approve of their husbands having naked girls posing about the house!

Looking back on what I did, it seems stupid. But I wanted to do it and I have managed it.

I am not anywhere yet, really – but I am aiming to shoot the centrefold of *Playboy!*

It was in 1951, on a boat to Malaya, that I first became interested in photography. I was a regular serviceman – one of the idiots that signed on!

An Ensign Ful-Vue was my first camera, soon followed by an Agfa Isolette. I found out all about developing and printing films in the RAF station photographic section as a sort of hobby.

This hobby continued after I left the services. At first, I could only make contact prints from the roll-film negatives, but persistent hints finally produced the much-needed enlarger as a present one Christmas.

Early subjects were the usual family snaps and landscapes. People liked the sort of work I was doing, though, and I soon started receiving requests from neighbours to photograph their babies and kids.

From these beginnings, I progressed to photographing girls from the typing pool at work. I am not too sure of the connection. I just fancied women, I suppose!

So far, all my indoor pictures had been taken with a single photoflood bulb in a small Photax reflector. This was fitted with a clip, so that it could be attached to the back of a chair, or shelf.

Something a little more professional was obviously called for, so I found two large tins, stuck a pole in each and filled them with concrete. Then I bought another clip-on reflector to go with these new lighting stands.

One of my very first glamour sessions was on a *Photo News Weekly* outing to Hastings. We had great times on the beach, though you took pot luck on the weather.

I submitted some of my beach shots to *Photo News Weekly* shortly after – and one of them was published.

It was this success which encouraged me to answer an advertisement in *Photo News Weekly*. "Photographer by the sea," ran the heading. "Would you like to be the staff photographer on a woman's magazine?"

My application was successful and I moved down to Bournemouth early in 1960.

Miss World and magazines

Within a couple of weeks of joining the magazine, I had a row with the editor about covering a local beauty contest.

"You're a woman's magazine," I argued. "If a local girl wins, it's good publicity. Why are you haggling about it?"

In the end, the editor agreed. "But don't make a meal of it," he warned.

It was at this contest that I first met Ann Sidney, who went on to become Miss World!

But things were not going so well for the magazine. One day, I got a call from the editor. "Howard, you are a luxury I can no longer afford," he said. "Go out and get yourself a job. When I've got more money, I'll take you back."

So it was back to office work. But at least I now had a few contacts. I continued to photograph Ann Sidney, and she was the subject of my first cover success with *Amateur Photographer.*

However, when Ann won the Miss World title, I lost my model. But quite a lot of my work had been published by now and was getting known. I actually had girls coming and asking me to photograph them!

By today's standard, my photographic sessions with Ann Sidney would hardly qualify for the glamour label. There were no topless shots. But a new model agency opened in Bournemouth and I hired two or three of the girls, submitting the pictures to magazines such as *Parade.*

Then I started having some success with *Spick, Span* and *Beautiful Britons* publications. I was receiving commissions from them nearly every week – the old stockings-and-suspender stuff mostly.

Every commission came with a shooting script. This was fine to a point, though it became a bit of a bore after a while.

But the shooting sessions could always be relied on to liven up the area. I remember one where I was photographing a local beauty queen riding a bike.

The first part went as planned. I put a small stone down on the road so that there was something for me to focus the camera on. Then I told her to ride slowly by with her right foot on the handle bars and the left foot down on the pedals. She had to show her briefs, you see. And as she passed over the small stone, I pressed the shutter release to capture the picture.

Then we came to the last shot, where it had to look as if she had fallen off the bike. She sat on the road and I lowered the bike on top of her. She lay spreadeagled, showing all she had got. And just as I was about to take a picture, a tractor and trailer with a load of hay came round the corner of the country lane. So I had to lift the bike up and drag her to her feet. We stood there on the side of the road while he drove past very slowly, staring at us as if we were something off another planet – he just could not believe what he had seen.

He kept looking and looking – until he drove straight into a ditch – tractor, trailer, hay and all!

I put the girl back on the ground, took the final picture and then cleared off home as quickly as possible.

Originally, very few of these magazines featured nude or topless models. It was mostly glimpses of underwear which quickened the pulses of purchasers.

Then a new type of magazine started to appear – and the girls they featured were definitely not wearing briefs and bra. Or much else!

Some of the magazines I was working for felt they had to offer their customers a little more, but I decided I did not want to get involved. Some of the requests were bordering on pornography and I did not want my girls getting into that kind of work.

Model girls and fees

So now I was on my own again. There was no magazine finding models for me, and no ready market for my photographs. I had to work hard to build up both areas.

These days, a lot of girls arrive through personal recommendation. One of my recent sessions, for example, was with a friend of my favourite model.

But I still scan pages of local papers for winners of beauty competitions. Usually, the name and address is given, so you can look through the telephone directory for their number. I phone them up and invite them round to meet my wife and have a look at some of my photographs.

Sometimes, I get girls writing to me after seeing one of my photographs in print. Now, though, I follow the view that sales are going to be low if you use the girl-next-door. The more professional the girl, the better your chances of selling some of the photographs. A professional model knows all about make-up and posing – she probably saves you money in the long run. But you cannot always afford to pay a professional.

Some time ago, I put a proposition to a local model agency. "Look," I said, "I can't afford to hire your girls, but if you'd like to send them to me for a photo session, I'll supply a whole portfolio of pictures – providing I can also sell these photographs for publication."

The arrangement worked well for a while – until the agency closed down. Now I have a similar arrangement with an agency in Bristol. Their new girls come to me free in return for photographs. If the girls have been modelling for a while, then I pay them about £50 for a day, and also supply a few pictures. For an established model, I have to pay the full day's fee.

Bournemouth might seem a long way for a Bristol girl to travel when she is not being paid very much, but the set-up seems to be working very well. The only problem is that the girl will not turn up if she is suddenly offered another assignment for more money. You almost come to expect the phone call from her before it arrives. It is a bonus if the girl turns up.

£100 for a day with a good model is a reasonable figure. If the girl is doing "page 3" work and I sell one picture, then I am in profit. And that is just from one shot – you can do a lot in a day. Of course, if you have got a mediocre model, then you are gambling.

However, I do not part with £100 for every photo session. If I am photographing an inexperienced local girl, then she does not get paid at all. It is another of my arrangements.

After the session, all the girl gets is a set of contact sheets from all the films shot, so that she can choose a few free prints. But whenever I sell any of these photographs, she gets 40% of the fee.

Some people may frown on this system, but I prefer it from a financial point of view.

In some ways, it can also give you better pictures. If you are paying a girl for the day, she may start clock-watching towards the end. You will not always get the best out of her during the last hour. However, if the girl knows that every photograph you take could mean more money, then you are going to keep her attention until the last minute.

Of course, one problem with this percentage method is that girls tend to move from one town to another. But it is up to the models to keep in touch with me and forward their latest address.

Some girls can also be a bit impatient. They see their photograph in print and expect the money to arrive a couple of days later. It does not work like that. It can be a month or more before the magazine pays the reproduction fee, and it can take even longer to reach me if the photograph was sold through my agent.

The girl just has to learn to wait. She is paid as soon as I have been paid.

Advantages of an agent

Is it worth using an agent to sell your photographs?

I think so. Maybe it is a gamble, but I have been with one now for fifteen years and I am quite happy.

My agent takes 45% of the fees earned by the photographs (most take 50%). Out of this comes all his expenses, so I get a clear 55% of the reproduction fee.

An agent is particularly useful if you produce work that might sell overseas. I do not have any contacts abroad, and if you post photographs to foreign magazines, there is a risk that they might be used without you being any the wiser.

Through my agent, I have recently had several pictures published in a South African magazine I had never heard of. The fee was £208. I would sooner have 55% of that than nothing at all.

As you might guess, I have a special arrangement with my agent. After each photo session, I produce two sets of contact sheets. The girl has one set and I keep the other. I make enlargements of all the photographs that might sell to photographic magazines and local papers, and I print up the pictures the model wants. Then the negatives go off to my agent and I forget all about them.

If I have been shooting transparencies, I keep back any I can handle, and then send the remainder off to him.

I deal direct with the photographic magazines, where I have good contacts. They do not pay big money – not like a daily paper, for example – but I have got to know some of these magazines quite well over the years, so my agent is quite happy to let me carry on with them.

Anyway, I like to feel that I am doing something. It is nice to have an agent who is selling abroad, and maybe to the national papers, but I like to do a bit myself. Then I feel that I am on the right road.

I am also selling direct to some of the puzzle magazines at the moment. I have made a break into one or two and now they ring me up and ask for certain types of picture – winter photographs and things like that.

It is nice when you get people asking for your work. Some time ago, *Amateur Photographer* called to say that they had some of my pictures and would I write an article to go with them. By the next Friday! It turned out that my feature was for a special glamour issue which included work by Patrick Lichfield.

How do you find yourself an agent?

I simply wrote to several that were listed in the *Writers' and Artists' Yearbook.* I found an agent, then dropped him because I was producing work that kept coming back. It was not right for any of his markets. But I went back to him when I started using girls that suited

Seventeen years separate these photographs of former Miss World Ann Sidney. Above is Ann at eighteen, before she won the title. On the left, looking even more glamorous is Ann in 1979, during another photo session with Ken Howard. So do not believe anyone who says that only girls in their late teens or early twenties can be glamour models.

These three colour shots have one photographic technique in common — all show backlighting.

It is almost impossible to take good glamour photographs when the girl is facing into the sun. She will not be able to look into the bright light, and the shadows from the direct illumination will be dark and hard-edged.

Shooting with the sun behind the model overcomes these problems. It also produces the attractive halo of light around her hair.

However, backlighting can mean that there is too little light on the front of the girl. The simplest way to overcome this drawback is with a large white reflector positioned just outside the camera's view. This will bounce back more than enough light to give good detail in the face and clothes. Ken Howard positioned a white reflector close to Carolyn Evans for all of these pictures.

This 'April shower' is nothing more than spray from a garden sprinkler. But the backlit water droplets provide an added attraction to the shot. Semi-clothed girls soaked in water can be unusually erotic and this type of picture is in constant demand. Some picture agencies even have a 'wet-look' classification. No glamour portfolio is complete without a few of these shots.

his clients.

Of course, an agent is not always right. After one photo session with a new girl, I sent my photographs off as usual, and was surprised when they all came back. "Don't like her," said my agent. "She won't sell."

I disagreed and started submitting the photographs direct to magazines. So far, one has appeared on the cover of a puzzle magazine, while another has been used by *Amateur Photographer.*

It is just one of those things. What my agent likes and what I like are two different things. But he knows his markets better than I do.

I certainly recommend an agent, if you are producing enough work. It is very expensive dealing direct with magazines, even in terms of postage. And then you have to buy several copies of each magazine, to see what they are using, and to try and follow their styles.

For me, that is too cumbersome. It is too expensive an operation.

Following leads

I am always scanning the local and national newspapers for stories which might offer a fresh face for my glamour photography. Here is an example of just one incident which illustrates the value of following up a simple lead.

There was an article in the *News of the World* about a blonde girl who has been deaf since the age of five, when she had meningitis. It finished by saying that she wanted to be a model, but that no professional photographer would spare the extra time needed to show her how to pose in front of a camera.

Well, I have lived next door to deaf and dumb people for fifteen years, so I am used to communicating with them. And I liked the look of the girl from her photograph in the paper.

Fortunately, I know one of the photographers on the *News of the World* and he agreed to give me a reference if I wrote to the editor. So I sent a letter to the newspaper, asking if they would put me in touch with the girl.

The result was that the girl came down one Saturday with her mother and father. After about half-an-hour, they realised everything was satisfactory and went off into Bournemouth. The two of us worked solidly for the rest of the day. We had not really finished by the time her parents came back in the evening.

The communication problem was nil. I showed her how to pose and turn. She picked up ideas quickly. I got a beautiful set of pictures from the session.

As soon as my agent received the shots, he placed one with the *Sunday Mirror.* They ran a story about her being a member of a rhythmic gymnastic team – quite a feat for a girl who cannot hear the music.

Then there was some trouble because she was a finalist in a beauty contest, and the organisers had not known she was deaf. They tried to drop her from the finals, but the *Sunday Mirror* picked this up and ran another story – using another of my photographs. I ended up giving my views about the whole thing on local radio, too.

She has now appeared on the cover of *Amateur Photographer* and the cover of a puzzle magazine, and she is going to be one of my big sellers. And all this came from a story I happened to see in the *News of the World.*

Remember this next time you throw the Sunday papers away. If you see something, follow it up. This business is all about getting off your backside and doing some work. If you just sit there thinking, you will never do anything.

I have always believed in one thing. If you want something, you ask for it. There are only two answers – yes and no. If the answer is no, hard luck. If it is yes, that is a bonus.

This is the way I like to work.

Cameras and accessories

My early Agfa Isolette camera was soon replaced by a series of twin-lens reflex models. A Rolleicord VA was the first, followed by one of the Rolleiflex cameras. Then two Mamiya-

flex C2 models led to my present Hasselblad 500CM.

I do not use 35mm very much – I have always been a large-format man. I used to have a Konica camera for holiday pictures, but I gave this to my son-in-law in return for decorating the kitchen. I hardly ever used it for glamour. Now if I need 35mm, I borrow my wife's Olympus Trip.

A Hasselblad is the camera most amateur photographers would like to own, but few can afford it. I would not have one now if I was not making money by selling photographs – not at the price they are today. You are talking about well over £1000 for the camera body, 80mm lens and the 150mm Sonar.

But I keep one of the old Mamiyaflex cameras, which still gets used from time to time. I had a problem with the Hasselblad at a wedding recently, so it pays to keep a second camera, just in case.

For studio work, I use a Bowens 400 outfit – two electronic studio flash heads, brollies and snoot. Most of my pictures are taken with just these two lights, though I sometimes supplement the set-up with an old Braun EF3 flash pack.

I bought this Braun for £25 about ten years ago from a professional photographer who was selling up. In addition to the main gun, it has an extension head with a nine-foot cable.

The main head of the Braun gets used for halo lighting.

It is taped to a stand – a pole fixed in a tin of concrete. I have made a cardboard shield which fits round the reflector and cuts down the area covered by the flash, and there are different gels which can be fitted in front to give coloured haloes round the head of the girl.

Anyone who has tried setting up a studio at home will have discovered one of the main problems of an average lounge. The light-coloured walls and ceiling bounce a lot of light around, making it difficult to control special effects. At first, I found it impossible to keep a black background black. But now I have the answer.

I have two 8 x 4 foot pieces of hardboard which I have painted dark brown. I wedge them either side of the room, about four or five feet from the background. They stop the light bouncing around quite so much. If the two studio flash units, with their brollies, are positioned right to the sides of the room, the light from these is shielded from the background by the hardboard. The result is a background which is really black.

For backlighting, I use both heads of the Braun EF3 unit, one on either side of the background, pointing in towards the back of the girl. Here, the hardboard has another use – it stops the backlights shining directly into the camera lens.

It all works very well. The only problem is moving the hardboard about – it is heavy!

For backgrounds, I use Colorama paper. I have about six rolls, in different colours. It is not cheap, but it is no use trying to make do with sheets. You need the proper thing.

Avoiding creases in the paper is the main problem – you cannot throw them out of focus very much in a small room. At first, I used to lay the roll of paper on the floor at the foot of the wall and lift the loose end up to the ceiling. The paper was held in place by nails.

But then there were so many holes in the wall that I was frightened the plaster would fall out! Now I use proper background stands. I have only had these a short time, but they are fantastic. Previously, there was a limit to how far I could run the heavy roll of paper along the floor. There was a crockery unit on one side and a fireplace on the other which got in the way.

But now it is the heavy roll of paper which is supported on the stand and the loose end which runs along the floor. I can cut the paper away round the fireplace so that there is a complete floor covering. This means that the girl can come further away from the background.

I lengthen the life of the Colorama paper by having another 8 x 4 foot sheet of hardboard on the floor under the background. This stops models in high-heeled shoes from punching dozens of little holes through to the carpet.

One accessory which is invaluable is a flash meter, though this gave me problems at first.

I found that it was fine for black-and-white film, but always gave me underexposed transparencies. I now open up half-a-stop for transparency films, and the results are perfect.

Finding different studio props can be a problem for anyone just starting glamour photography. One answer is to buy furniture for the home which can also be used for glamour photography. This hanging chair, for example, looks as if it is suspended from the ceiling, but is actually supported by a floor-standing frame. It's the sort of chair which could be found a place in many homes, and it is an ideal accessory for glamour sessions. One alternative is to borrow furniture from a local shop, perhaps in exhange for display photographs of the items.

This is Ken Howard's home studio. It is in this confined area that he produces nearly all his indoor shots. Two studio flash units provide most of the light.

Another useful item is the Polaroid back which I have just bought for my Hasselblad camera. I can shoot a Polaroid picture and see the result within a minute to check lighting effects. The print often shows up faults which might otherwise be missed, saving valuable transparency film.

Other accessories include a soft-focus filter, though I do not use this much.

When it comes to the actual photo session, I usually have a few ideas about what I want, but rarely shoot with any specific magazine in mind. I set up the background and maybe a few props, and then let the session develop as the model begins to pose.

Later on, I will spend an evening going through the contact sheets and the pictures will throw up an idea for an article. Sometimes I will write a feature and send it off with the photographs, sometimes I will phone an editor and ask if he might be interested in anything on that theme.

One area where I have not done very well is in competitions. I have only won prizes in about three. I always read the rules carefully, so it must be that my pictures are not what the judges are looking for. I often come close to winning, but not near enough for my liking.

I will keep on trying.

This is Ken Howard's home studio. It is in this confined area that he produces nearly all his indoor shots. Two studio flash units provide most of the light.

*A deserted beach?
Probably not. But if you shoot
towards the sea, none of the
people stopping to watch are
likely to get in the way.*

Tom Hustler is one of Britain's leading society photographers. He has been commissioned to do royal sittings, and numerous weddings.

His background is very much that of the people he photographs — Eton, the army and the Stock Exchange. But then he broke away and joined a photographic studio as an assistant.

After many years in London, Tom Hustler moved to Reading, where he now lives in a house which has been converted to his photographic requirements. A small studio area fights for space with his economical office, while his darkroom is tucked away in a garden shed!

These facilities are no greater than those enjoyed by many amateur photographers — but few can match Tom's range of work.

His photographs have appeared in many different forms for many different purposes — theatre programmes, record sleeves, advertisements, newspaper features — but there is always one common feature. People. Tom Hustler photographs them young and old, famous and infamous — and glamorous. In the next few pages, he gives good advice for anyone wanting to follow in his footsteps.

"How did you become a professional photographer?" is a question I am asked time and again.

Well, to start near the beginning, I was educated at Eton. I had no say in the matter. It was the natural progression from a house with a nursery wing and a butler.

At Eton, I excelled at pottery! But I was hopeless at games and only average at studies.

I was drafted into the army for National Service and eventually became an officer, joining the Somerset Light Infantry in Malaya.

It was out there that I first became interested in photography. One of my friends had some old copies of *Amateur Photographer* and I used these to learn about shutter speeds and apertures, film speeds and exposures.

I took shots of local scenes with my Zeiss Ikonta M camera and used the photographs to illustrate my letters home. I was an amateur photojournalist!

Back in England, my enthusiasm for photography waned. Subjects at home seemed very ordinary when compared with scenes from the Far East.

By day, I was a trainee clerk with a firm of London stockbrokers. By night, I did the rounds of the deb dance circuit (I needed the food, and enjoyed the free champagne and female company!).

I began taking photographs again, mostly of girl-friends. My studio was a room in the flat I shared, with illumination from two simple floodlamps. I taught myself lighting by copying styles from the photographs I found in books and magazines.

Developing and printing was done under the stairs, with wet films and prints hung over the bath to dry.

After two years of City drudgery, I decided to leave the Stock Exchange and work as a photographer. It was a big step to take, although I had a little money to start me off.

I struggled along, working from a house in Chelsea. But although I was taking photographs of a reasonable standard, I was not selling them.

Then, through a friend, I had the chance to meet Tony Armstrong-Jones, now Lord Snowdon. He took a long look at my amateurish efforts and gave the following advice.

"Get together some more samples and get a job with an established studio, even if you are paid very little. You need to learn the professional side."

It is advice which I would echo to anyone today.

With some difficulty, I managed to obtain the job of darkroom boy in Dorothy Wilding's studio. This was ideal for me, as she specialised in society portraiture, and was also a famous royal photographer.

It turned out that Dorothy Wilding had taken me on because she thought I was well-connected and would bring in a lot of new business. She was wrong! After six months, she realised her mistake and offered to sell me the business. I bought it.

In addition to the formal portraits, I started shooting parties and dances for magazines like *The Tatler* and *Queen,* and began having some of my work published in newspapers.

I was asked to shoot formal and informal photographs for some of Dorothy Wilding's old clients, including Dukes and Duchesses. I began shooting publicity pictures for stage productions at London theatres. And to fill the quiet winter months, I tried glamour photography.

The professional approach

Glamour photography is the art of capturing pretty girls looking their best – or better than their best! Success depends on the skill of the photographer and the looks and professionalism of the model.

A professional photographer's approach is straightforward. He will contact the top model agencies to find the most suitable girls for the type of work he wants to do. He will probably want to see a portfolio of their pictures, and may ask them along for an audition, or to discuss the work.

A top glamour photographer does not waste time. He has his studio, lights and props ready in advance. Equally, a top model will arrive a little early. She will put the finishing touches to her appearance and be ready to start the session on time.

Photographer and model will work together as a team during shooting, each adding suggestions and ideas for the different poses and situations. In one session, they will often produce a variety of photographs suitable for sale to different markets.

Any glamour photographer – amateur or professional – must strive for this professionalism. If you hire a studio and use a top model, you have a better chance of producing saleable shots than if you photograph a girl-friend in the lounge.

But it is best to build up skill, technique and experience before you spend money on expensive studios and models.

Family portraits

It is essential to practice taking pictures of people. This will help you to learn how to use your camera quickly, efficiently, and with the minimum of fuss.

If you have not already reached this stage, practice taking flattering portraits of family and friends.

I say "flattering," because this is what glamour is all about. Few models even try to look as sexy and attractive in real life as they do in photographs. Also, they are unlikely to wear such provocative clothes when walking down the high street, or pose in the positions they use for the camera!

A good example of this was the time my wife and I went to a beach in the south of France. When she was walking around or sunbathing in a mini-bikini, she attracted only the normal amount of attention for a pretty girl. But when she started posing for my camera at the edge of the sea, a huge crowd of people suddenly appeared.

You may have to ask your family sitters to take up slightly unnatural positions to achieve the flattering results you want.

Say you are taking portraits of a thirty-year-old aunt. This is not an easy age – they always think that they look younger.

First, ask her to wear a plain, simple polo-neck jumper, or a blouse – bare shoulders and patterned dresses are difficult to photograph well.

Then make sure that her hair is tidy, that skin blemishes are covered with a light foundation cream, and that her eyes are exaggerated by make-up.

Pose her with shoulders turned away from the camera, which should be above the level of her eyes. If she is tall, sit her on a low stool, or stand on a box yourself. Use a telephoto lens, if possible, so that you are at least four feet away. Ask her to straighten her back, lean forward and turn towards the camera, keeping her chin down with eyes looking into the lens.

You will have to get a good expression by chatting to her. Simply saying what you want to see seldom works, except with professional models.

Indoors, position the main light so that she is facing it. This is a flattering light, exaggerating the eyes and mouth. It also eliminates, or at least reduces, any "bags" under the eyes (unless the light is too high), and it shows cheek bones to their best advantage.

If you have a second light, use it to illuminate the hair from behind, but do not let this spill over to the face or background.

If the main light is harsh, soften the shadow side with a lamp which is less bright, or use a reflector to throw some of the main light back.

Outdoors, find a location away from direct sunlight, but where there is lovely soft frontal light. Use the reflection from a light-coloured wall, or sit your subject in the shade under a tree, facing a bright patch of sky. Try to find a plain dark background, such as an out-of-focus hedge.

If you can take good photographs under these conditions, you are ready to make a start with glamour photography.

Find a model

Good subjects for glamour photography are not easy to find. You need a pretty girl with an attractive face and thinner-than-average figure. It will help if she knows something about

This is a stock shot — a photograph which is taken with no specific market in mind, but which might appeal to a wide range of newspapers and magazines. Amateur Photographer *was one of the magazines which used this picture. Stock shots should be sent to picture agencies and publishers, and then be forgotten about. If the photographs are good, money will start to trickle in after a few months — and could still be flowing after ten years! Few photographers make a living from stock shots, but the extra money means jam for the bread-and-butter.*

make-up technique, and can change her hair-style easily and quickly.

Do not rely on chance for your encounters with potential models. Go out and look for them. Young actresses and beauty queens are just two groups of girls who probably have the looks and poise needed for pictures – and they may also welcome a few free publicity photographs.

When you find a face you would like to photograph, be careful of your next move. An approach which is too direct may make her apprehensive.

Have some simple cards printed with your name, address, telephone number, and possibly the words 'freelance photographer.' Give the girl one of your cards, say that you

Sunglasses are a good stand-by for any swimsuit shot. They give the girl something to do with her hands. You will find that hands are one of the most difficult parts of the body to pose. Often, hiding the hands is the easiest answer. If this is not possible, you can often get the girl to pretend she is buttoning her blouse, or tying her bikini.

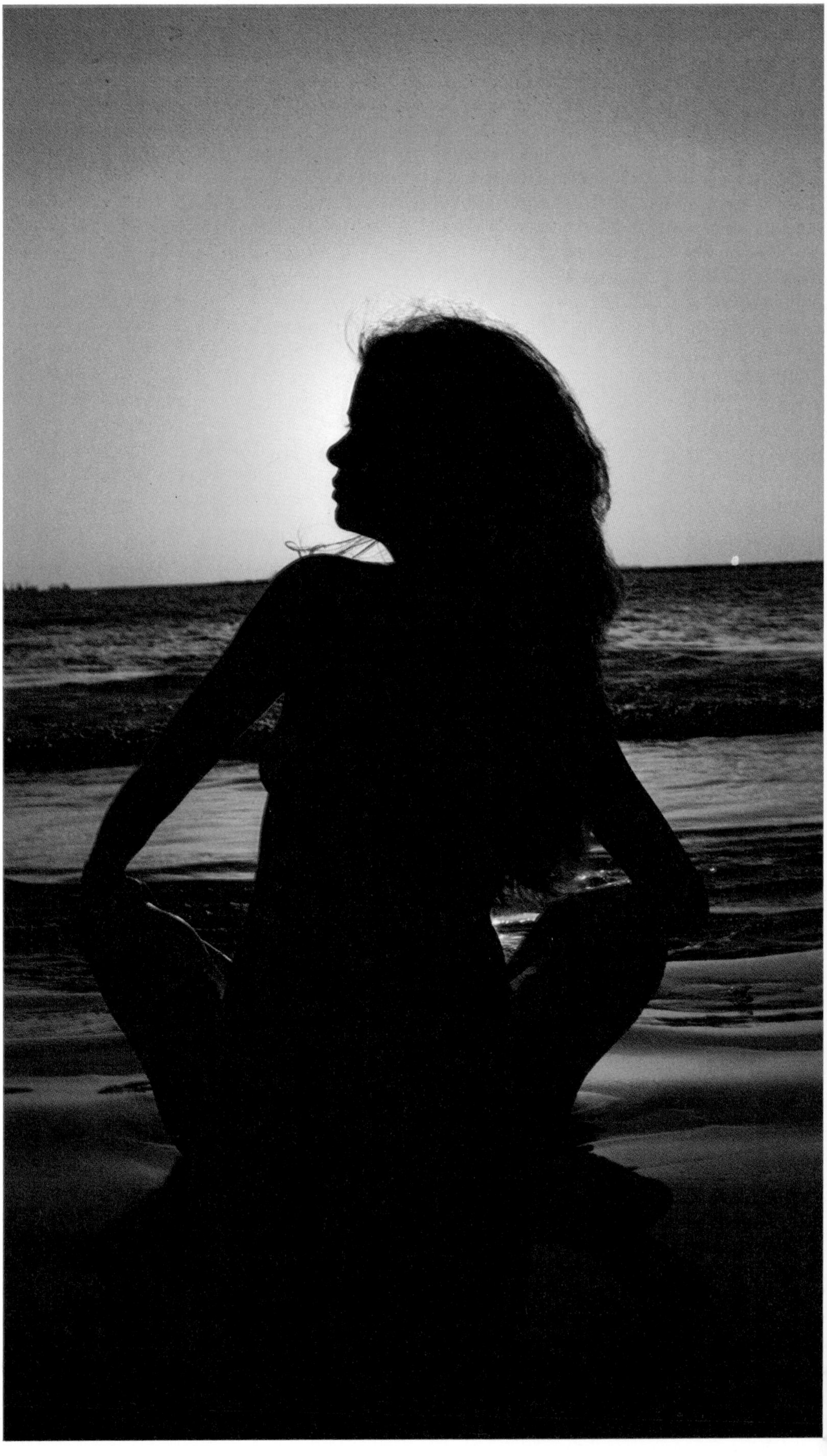

would like to take some photographs, and then wait for her to get in touch with you.

You may not hear from some of the girls, but the more cards you put out, the more chances you have of finding new models.

If you are married to someone who wants to help with your photography, she may be able to find models for you – but most wives are not too keen on their husbands taking up glamour photography.

Put the word round at work, or in the pub, or your club, that you are looking for pretty girls for portrait modelling, and are willing to provide some free pictures. There are quite a few proud dads and boyfriends around who might be able to offer you an introduction.

A few years ago, I spotted a very attractive girl serving behind the bar in a pub. I could not make contact over the bar, so I gave the landlord, who knew me well, a card for her, asking if she would come round to my studio to discuss a possible photographic session. She had never heard of me, but the landlord gave me a good reference. I not only found a super model, I found a wife!

The glamorous touch

Unless a girl makes the best of her looks before she sits in front of the camera, what chance has the photographer?

Everyday make-up may sometimes be satisfactory for colour portraiture, but it will not usually look so good in black-and-white. Ask the girl to use a light matt foundation, plenty of mascara, soft matt-brown eye shadow, and lipstick a little darker than her natural lip colour. She should add a little lip gloss, but no other shiny make-up, and no blushers or shading to start with.

If she arrives with a basic, simple make-up which accentuates the eyes and mouth, this will do well for your first black-and-white pictures. She can always add the blushers and shiny eye shadows later for colour pictures, or any special effects you want to try.

Sunsets can provide a dramatic backdrop for a glamorous girl. The richest colours come from exposing for the background, putting the subject in silhouette. This technique opens up markets which would not normally consider using a photograph of a nude figure — record album covers, for example.

Glamour photographs do not need to be logical — they are, after all, mostly about fantasies. So a girl giving a salute while wearing casual clothes and a military helmet is not going to raise many eyebrows. In fact, there is a good market for this type of shot, since the situation gives caption writers something to talk about!

Hair depends on the normal cut and style. Ask the girl to bring heated hair rollers, if she has them, for final styling in the studio.

Get as much width and bounce in the hair as possible, and keep it forward to frame the face. Let her try different styles with the hair during the sitting.

Make-up is not much help if the lighting does not add to the glamour. To find the best lighting, sit your model in the basic pose described earlier, turn on your main light and turn off all the other lights in the room. Draw curtains to exclude daylight, or pin black cloth over the windows.

Place the light close to the camera, but higher. With the girl looking straight into the lens, you should see a small shadow under her nose.

Look through the camera viewfinder and see how the light affects the face. Move the light down slowly, checking the effect all the time. You should find that a lower light brings out more of the eyes, but it also flattens and widens the appearance of the face.

Keeping the model in the same pose, move the light around to the other side of the camera, about a foot away from it, and repeat the experiment. No face is symmetrical, so light from this other side will give a slightly different result.

Now, with the light at camera height, start to move it slowly away from the camera, but at a constant distance of around four feet from the girl. Make a mental note of any lighting positions which seem to give attractive results.

If the model is sitting only a few feet from a background, her shadow may be in the picture if the light is low and close to the camera. It is not essential to eliminate this – sometimes a background shadow can add to the effect.

When you have found the best main light position, decide whether you need a fill-in light to soften the shadows on the side of her face which is not receiving direct illumination.

If your main light is very soft (from a large window, for example, or a flash umbrella), you may not need a fill-in light. If you do not have a second light, and the main light is harsh, keep it close to the camera to avoid heavy shadows.

Another light can be used on the hair, from behind the model. This is often called 'kick' lighting, and is very effective. Hair often photographs darker than natural, because it absorbs light, so this back lighting gives extra 'life.'

It also separates the girl from the background, giving an extra dimension to the photograph.

The 'kick' light is usually a spotlight, or a flashhead fitted with a snoot. It is placed behind and above the model, shining down on her hair, but not spilling over on the face. I sometimes put my backlight directly behind the model's head – this gives a rim-lighting halo effect.

Directing the session

It is your job to direct the model into the poses, mood and facial expressions you want.

You will find this difficult at first. You may feel that you know what you want, but are unable to explain this to her. And she may be as awkward and shy as you are!

The best way round this problem is to explain what you are trying to achieve, and discuss this with her. Show her glamour portraits you have cut from magazines and put in a scrapbook – this will provide basic poses from which you can develop your own ideas.

Expressions should be natural, attractive and slightly alluring. The eyes can make or ruin a photograph, which is why I concentrate on them so much.

Get the model to work directly into the camera lens. In the final picture, it will seem as if she is looking directly at the viewer. If the expression is gently provocative and sexy, the viewer will feel that she is eyeing him in that way.

When you are directing these expressions, keep looking through the camera viewfinder. When the pose and expression is almost right, shoot a couple of frames. Then vary the expression slightly by asking her to part the lips a little, move her chin down a bit, or turn her head round a fraction. You will gradually evolve your own style of directing, but try to keep chatting and do not ask her to hold a position for too long.

After you have taken successful glamour head-shots of about half-a-dozen girls, you should have built up enough skill and confidence to move on to the next stage. This is three-quarter and full-length glamour photography.

Plan your first session for outdoors, if possible. Ask the girl to bring along a variety of clothing, from swimwear to shirts and shorts. High boots look good with shorts, and shirts can be pulled up to reveal a bare middle.

As soon as you start to photograph the full length of your model, you encounter many more problems. You will have to tell her how to stand, what to do with her hands, which way to twist her body and head, when to bend a knee – everything, in fact.

Glamour poses are meant to look reasonably natural. At the same time, they must be provocative, showing off the girl's figure in the best way. An attractive girl in a brief bikini climbing out of a swimming pool will look sexy, but if she is wearing a thin wet shirt which clings to her breasts and is smiling seductively into the camera, the result will be more suggestive.

It is impossible to describe every possible pose – and a waste of time. Each girl is an individual and will look different even when adopting a standard pose. A pose which works for one girl will look ridiculous with another.

Posing outdoors should not be too difficult, because the girl can make use of natural props in the location. Let her lean against a tree, a wall or a lawn-mower. On the beach, she can sit on a breakwater. In gardens and parks, trees and benches are useful settings.

But try to keep backgrounds as simple and uncluttered as possible, and only introduce props gradually as you learn how to handle them. Remember that the girl is more important.

In my studio, I usually start by asking the girl to face the main light while turning her shoulders away and twisting her hips towards it. Then I ask her to lift the foot on the far side from the camera and swing it around in front of the nearest knee.

Hands can look very ugly if they are big. They can be kept down by the sides with the elbows slightly bent, or lifted with the thumbs tucked into the tops of trousers or shorts. Hands look more elegant if they are seen sideways to the camera.

If the model has good hands and nails, I often get her to put one hand up to her face with a fingertip placed in the corner of her slightly open mouth. This often produces a lovely cheeky expression.

In the studio, lighting is much the same as for head shots, but keep experimenting with different positions, so that there is some variety in your pictures.

Outdoors, photographing full-length may make it more difficult for you to make use of reflected light from a wall. If so, use a small electronic flash to fill-in the shadow detail.

Cameras and equipment

Start with the equipment you already have, learn to use it quickly and efficiently, and only change when it cannot do what you want.

I use Rollei twin-lens reflex cameras for my black-and-white work. Black-and-white roll film is easier to handle in the darkroom than 35mm, and the larger format leads to a print quality which is more marketable.

For colour transparencies, I use Kodachrome 64 film in a 35mm Canon single-lens reflex camera.

The choice of film is always personal. Most well-known brands are good, so pick just one make of film in each type (black-and-white, colour negative and colour transparency), and learn what it will do for you. When you appreciate the qualities, you will be able to rely on it. Do not change from one film to another unless you become unhappy with the results.

The rule for accessories is, the fewer the better. Apart from your standard camera lens, all you need is a medium telephoto for portrait work. Lens hoods for all the lenses are essential, and it is worth having an ultra-violet or haze filter if you work on beaches or at high altitudes. Add a tripod, and maybe a separate light meter, plus a sturdy bag to keep everything in.

Photographers who walk round looking like Christmas trees do not usually take very good photographs. At one lecture I was giving, someone suggested that it would be a good

High-key illumination is good for glamour portraits. Very few models have perfect skin, so flat lighting helps to hide any small spots or lines. The high-key effect is produced by positioning the main light very close to the camera, almost on a line with the axis of the lens. Then you place one or more white reflectors close to the face, just outside the camera's field-of-view. You may need to light the hair separately.

idea to carry a reflector for outdoor portraiture. Nonsense! It is much better to find a natural reflector, such as a light-coloured wall.

Around 1959, Tony Armstrong Jones and the late Dorothy Wilding were being interviewed on television. Tony said: "I like to try and take pictures by natural light from sky or windows." Miss Wilding replied, "Mr. Jones, in my studio, I can put the sun where I want it."

Nobody can rely on the weather in this country, so you will have to buy some sort of indoor lighting equipment eventually. The cheapest way is to try and find secondhand photofloods through advertising, or by asking around at your local camera club.

I started with lights like that to take pictures of girlfriends in my flat. I even sold pictures from successful sittings at 1s 6d each (it was in 1955!).

When I joined Dorothy Wilding later, she used huge floodlights and spotlights. It was only years later that suitable electronic equipment was developed for my type of work.

A large floodlight, and small flood and a spotlight, all on stands, will be a good basic starter kit. The floods can be used for main and fill-in light, while the spot makes a good hair light.

Normally, these lights will only be big enough and sufficiently powerful for head-and-shoulder portraits, and perhaps half-length poses. Even then you will have to use fast film and slow shutter speeds.

However, these photoflood lamps do show exactly what you are going to get on the film. Photography is all about painting with light and shadow – these lights are your brushes.

Many photographers use small electronic flashguns for portraits, perhaps firing them into a small white umbrella to diffuse the light. Unfortunately, there is no way to see the results produced by the flash until the film is processed. At this stage, I think it is better to stay with the photofloods.

The next step is to buy a mains-powered electronic flash with a built-in modelling light. This can be used with a variety of umbrellas and reflectors – but it is only a single light source. You really need two or three of these studio flash units for varied results.

The great advantage of electronic flash lighting is high power with soft illumination. The duration of the flash is very short – less than 1/1000 sec – which removes the problems of camera shake and model movement. In fact, a model's action or expression can be 'frozen' in a way which is impossible to achieve with photoflood lighting.

Indoors, a plain white, grey or blue wall is ideal for glamour photography, and it reproduces well in newsprint. I made a dark background by taking a 4 x 5 foot piece of red velvet to two broom handles – it hangs from a picture hook!

Avoid patterned wallpapers unless you can throw them well out of focus.

Selling your shots

An important part of selling is called 'market research.' If you are putting together a scrapbook of glamour pictures from the magazines and newspapers you buy, then you have already started researching.

Look at how different publications use different types of pictures. Show pages use glamour girls, for example, but only if the girl has appeared, or is about to appear, in a film or television series. Some papers use topless shots, others prefer more modest pictures. Some like newsy captions, others are happy with just a few background details.

Do not forget that pictures lose quality when reproduced, so keep the lighting strong and clear, and produce sharp and punchy prints.

For newspapers, remember that the poses must fit into an upright column – few papers use horizontal shots. And keep arms and legs close to the body, so that they do not get chopped off in print!

Glamour photography is a fantasy for the viewer. Any normal male likes looking at pictures of pretty girls. They may be out of reach, and he may never meet a girl who looks like that, but he can always hope or dream about such a meeting. That is what sells the magazines and newspapers which use these pictures.

Although you can start to take pictures with just one basic lighting set-up, a good glamour photographer knows how to use lighting for effect. Here, two lights have been used from the sides to emphasise the slim shape of Vanessa Brooks. The side lighting throws a shadow down the back of the model. It is the smooth curve of this shadow which makes the shot so attractive. Flat frontal lighting would have produced a pointless picture.

Six photographers/Harvey Nielsen

A small terraced house in Gravesend, Kent, does not provide much space for a glamour studio. Harvey Neilsen, however, has overcome the problems and is currently carving out a share of the market.

Starting with photographs published in the local paper, Harvey has gone on to place work in newspapers and magazines around the world. Many of the girls who appear in his photographs are from the Gravesend area, spotted in local streets and shops. With Harvey's help, some have since gone on to successful modelling careers in London.

Glamour photography is only part of the work covered by this versatile photographer. Saturday afternoons in winter will often find him covering football matches for a sports agency, and he is also making a name for himself as a photographer at rock concerts.

One of my great hobbies as a child was watching the ships on the Thames and collecting pictures of them.

In those days, though, the photographs were expensive, so I hit on the idea of doing my own. A friend and I managed to obtain passes for the dockyards and we went around taking the shots we wanted.

These photographs were only for my own pleasure; I never tried to sell any. But it was the start of my interest in photography.

When I left school, I joined the Royal Navy. This gave me the opportunity to use my camera in foreign countries and my photography started to improve. I entered a few competitions and had some success, winning my very first single lens reflex camera – an Exa.

Then I had the chance to buy myself out of the Navy, which I did. Photography was the only thing I thought I was any good at, so I took a job on the service side, repairing cameras and projectors.

Like everyone else, I also did some extra work in my spare time. One of my clients was a studio which wanted their cameras serviced regularly. After a while, they suggested that I might like to make use of their studio.

My first session went well and I showed the results to the studio manager. He thought it was very good and suggested that I have a go at selling some of the photographs.

The pictures were of pretty girls, so I sent a few to a *Reveille*-type magazine. They sold, and I used the money to pay for another photo session. I made money from these pictures, too, and began to do more and more freelance work. By now, I was service manager with the company which employed me, and I was able to borrow some very good cameras for my photographic assignments.

I started covering weddings – which I hated. But this brought me into contact with some of the local newspapers, and they asked if I did any other type of work. Well, I had been doing some sports photography, so I soon found myself covering local sports events as a freelance photographer.

Then I picked up a commission with Sport and General, one of the big London sporting picture agencies. I was photographing First and Second Division football matches for them.

I like covering sport, because it is immediate. You never get the chance to take the same photograph twice. Dramatic events usually happen in a brief moment of time – it is an achievement to capture a very good shot.

Pop concerts, which I also cover, are the same. You are never sure of what you are going to get.

Photographing a girl is different. The two of you are working together to produce a good photograph – a photograph which will sell tomorrow, next month or next year.

That is one of the big differences between sports photography and glamour photography. A good sports photograph may not be used because it does not happen to fit the page of a newspaper on a particular day. And if it is not used that day, it will not be used at all, because the photograph dates very quickly. Nobody wants to see last week's football match in next week's papers.

A glamour photograph, however, is less topical, and I found that local newspapers would use at least one a week. Pictures of girls seemed a lot easier to sell, so I concentrated on this area.

Eventually, I was turning down more and more photographic work because I could not fit it all into my spare time. Should I leave my job as service manager and become a full-time freelance photographer?

My divorce had come through, so there was only myself to think about. I did a little book work. I had about £1000 in the bank, which – as far as I was concerned – was enough to keep me going for six months. I decided to give it a go for six months, and then review the situation.

And really, I have just gone on from there.

Getting the girls

I started off by photographing friends of friends. Once a few of these pictures were published, it became a lot easier for me to walk up to a girl and ask if she would be interested in modelling.

It is not a small community in this area, but it is small enough for people to know what you are doing. I would give the girl my business card and leave her to phone me. And nine times out of ten, it worked.

A lot of girls like to be flattered, and taking photographs is a form of flattery – providing you can produce results.

The only unpleasant situations have been with girls who have taken up a similar offer, only to find that the photographer's intentions were less honourable than mine. You risk a very flat refusal here.

And I have had a pint of beer tipped over my head by a girl's boy-friend who was not too keen on the idea of his young lady working for me!

Luck has played its part, too. One of the picture agencies I work for was looking for some models on behalf of another glamour photographer. It was for a calendar assignment, and the client wanted girls who would not be appearing on other calendars that year.

The agency knew that I photographed local girls, and thought that I might know one or two that fitted the requirements. I sent along Jackie Jones and Suzy Watkins. Both got the job and have since gone on to bigger and better things.

The local paper, though, covered their calendar assignment, and my name received a good mention. The word spread that I could find good work for models, and girls started to approach me, rather than me approach them. I began to receive phone calls and letters from young hopefuls.

However, very few of the girls who call or write make it to the national papers, and even fewer are able to make a career from modelling. The girls that get on are usually the ones that I have found myself.

I still keep my eyes open. I am involved with local beauty contests and have found four or five successful girls from among the contestants.

The idea of modelling appeals to a lot of girls. With the high level of unemployment, attractive girls who are unable to find any other job are prepared to see if their face and figure will work for them.

The winner of a beauty contest, though, will not always be a good model. I have photographed girls who looked fantastic in front of the camera, but appeared very ordinary in the pictures. I have also worked with girls who would not get a second glance in the street, yet looked great in the photographs.

A photographic model is a very special breed of girl. I do not think you can teach modelling – if a girl has this ability, all you can do is bring it out.

It is this spark of ability that I look for when I am out and about. If I see a girl who might have it, I try to arrange a test photo session to see what comes out on film.

About ten of the girls I have found are now making good careers in modelling. In the past, there would come a stage where I was unable to help them any further, so I introduced them to established model agencies in London.

However, now that I am selling more and more of my work, I am coming into contact with a lot of other photographers. This means I have more opportunity to find the girls work. One girl on my books at the moment – Julie James – has worked with photographers like Sam Haskins and Barry Ryan.

At the moment, the model agency side of my business does not make a profit. However, I think it will make money once it is better established.

I would like to get more involved in the agency side, but I do not think I will end up behind a desk shepherding thirty or forty girls around to other photographers. I have too many ideas of my own about the type of shots that would suit a girl, and the sort of photographs I would like to see. I get a kick out of my own photography, and would hate to give it up.

This beautiful portrait relies on a hair net for its effect. The net has been placed over the face, rather like a delicate veil. Simple accessories like this attract the eye, making your photographs stand out from the crowd.

Selling the shots

If you are sending photographs to national newspapers and magazines, you must use top-line models. You will not sell pictures of an average-looking girl to the national press.

An exception to this is the glamour photograph with news content. A vicar's daughter who goes hang-gliding would be worth photographing, even if she was not as attractive as your usual models. Anything unusual will sell a photograph.

Using a flashgun on the camera is not normally the best way to light a glamour shot. Here, though, it works. This is mostly because the background is a good distance away from the girl, so there is no harsh shadow immediately behind her body. Flash on camera was used because of the difficulty in transporting studio flash to this setting — a discotheque. Although not much of the surroundings are shown, the photograph captures the clubland atmosphere. Locations like this are all around — you only have to ask permission to use them.

A straightforward glamour shot, though, needs a pretty girl – and this is one of the problems amateur photographers face. They work with amateur models to produce amateur photographs.

A local paper, however, might be interested in running a series of photographs of local girls. Here, you could sell pictures which would never make it in the national papers.

It is worth having a word with the editor of the local paper first, to see what they might require. I have yet to come across a local paper that will run topless shots. However, I would never submit a topless shot of a local girl to a local paper, because it could cause a lot of problems for her family and friends.

Usually, a local paper likes to see a covered pin-up pose. Swimwear looks a little dated these days – a cheesecloth shirt and shorts, maybe, looks a lot better.

Most of my work, though, goes through picture agencies. I deal with two, and they each work in different ways. The first agency is more of a library. They put your photographs into their files and wait for clients to come along with specific requirements. It can take a long time to sell pictures this way – you have to wait for a client who needs photographs similar to the ones you have taken.

The second agency is more interested in news and interest pictures which can be

This colourful head-dress was seen in a shop window and borrowed just for the photo session. At the start of the shooting, model Julie James was wearing bikini pants, but these looked wrong. Then one of the feathers fell from the head-dress and proved to be the perfect alternative.
If you go to a lot of trouble to set up shots like this, it makes sense to shoot in both black-and-white and colour. This gives you a much wider range of markets when you start to submit the photographs for publication.

sent out to newspapers and magazines. This is better for my sports pictures.

A lot of photographers resent paying the agency up to 50% commission on sales. However, a good agency will submit your work to publishers you have never heard of in countries across the world. I have made sales to Argentina, South Africa, Spain and France.

With black-and-white pictures, all you have to do is send the negatives to the agency. They make all the prints – which can be 20 x 16in for the national newspapers – and they write the captions. I think they offer good value for their commission fee.

Of course, if you have already submitted work direct to a publisher before sending the photographs to the agency, you must make this clear. There is nothing worse for an agent than to find that a set of 20 x 16in prints sent to a publisher had been rejected the week before.

If you are submitting colour, most agencies will want to see at least 200 transparencies – and these must not be all of the same girl! You must have variety, as well as quantity.

I normally like to take photographs for a specific market. Then I will take them along to that particular magazine or paper. If the publisher buys, I send all the extra pictures from the session to the agency, but only for publication abroad. If I am unable to make any sales myself, all the photographs go to the agency for syndication.

It is quantity which sells through an agency, rather than the single shot. The more photographs you have with an agent, the more chance you have of a regular monthly or quarterly cheque dropping through the letter-box.

Some of my early photographs, taken ten years ago, are still selling. I occasionally receive payment for pictures I cannot recall. The average life of a photograph, though, seems to be about two-and-a-half years. After this, I think the style of photography changes and the picture begins to look a little dated.

However, there are magazines that will suddenly want to show a flashback to the sixties, or use a style of photograph from the seventies. Or it could happen that a girl you photographed five years ago has suddenly become a celebrity and early pictures of her are in demand. You just do not know when your photographs will be wanted, or how often they will be used.

This means that the glamour shot which does not date has a much longer life than one which shows the current fashions. Fortunately, fashions seem to go round in circles. There was a trend at one stage for girls to have a rather frizzed and shaggy hairstyle. Some of my early shots of this have been selling again recently, as this style comes back in vogue.

Studio and equipment

My 'studio' is simply a room in my house. It is only about 12 feet square. If I want to move back any further, I have to shoot from the kitchen! It is a strange arrangement, but it works.

For basic lighting, I use two Courtenay Colourflash 100 studio flash units. Because the room is small, I find I can make use of a lot of reflected light from the white walls and ceiling. I have used additional small flashguns from time to time, but I get by with just the two studio units for most of my photography.

One light is usually used with a large gold umbrella at about 45 degrees from the camera. The wall on the opposite side to this main light acts as a reflector, softening the shadows.

The second light is aimed at the model or the background, depending on the type of effect I want.

I always use a flash meter to check the exposure, even though I know that it will always read around f/8. The meter also lets me experiment more with the lighting. I can decide to bounce the light from the ceiling to see what happens, and still produce correctly-exposed pictures.

I have also been experimenting with photographs taken by just the modelling lights, without flash. It gives a different feel to my black-and-white photographs, and I have had some interesting results using tungsten-light colour film and filters.

I think you can get too set in your ways at times. You must not be afraid to experiment a little. I know a lot of photographers who make a very good living using standard 'page 3' type lighting for every picture. They just walk into the studio, flick the light switches and start shooting.

That is not my style. I like to try to produce a little variety in my pictures. They may look similar when you see them all together, but there is something different between them at the time of shooting.

My studio backgrounds are standard rolls of background paper cut in half. This gives a paper width of about 4ft 6in. It is a very nice size – I find that the background just fills a 6 x 6cm transparency at the distances I normally shoot from. And I get two rolls of paper for the price of one!

At the moment, the background is supported on a Courtenay Mini Background System. This is a metal tripod stand with a metal trough at the top. It works very well, although the model will sometimes step back on the tripod legs and put a heel through the paper.

In the studio I am building upstairs, I am going to fit ring bolts in the ceiling and support the background from that. It will give me more flexibility.

I find that I can produce shadowless white backgrounds without any trouble. The main light is used at 45 degrees with an umbrella reflector. The second light is used from the opposite side and aimed directly at the background without an umbrella.

I have made my own 'barn door' to stop stray light from creeping back to the camera lens. However, I can also use the 'barn door' to let some of the light spill over the back of the model, giving a very attractive lighting effect.

Full-length shots would not seem possible in a studio of my size, but if I go through the kitchen and into the ground floor bathroom, I can still see the model! This lets me shoot full-length pictures with a 150mm lens on my Hasselblad. Usually, though, I switch to a 35mm lens on a Nikon or Nikkormat camera for full length photographs, as the wide-angle view means I can stay in the studio with the girl!

However, there is very little call for full-length pictures. Newspapers like to work with compact shapes. You can normally cut the image off at the knee, or put the girl in a kneeling or crouched pose.

For most of my 35mm photography, I use a 70-150mm zoom lens. These longer focal lengths give a very flattering perspective for glamour photography. I do not think you would be too successful using a standard camera lens. An 80mm or 90mm lens is ideal for anyone just starting 35mm glamour photography.

I am a firm believer in Kodak Tri-X for black-and-white roll-film work. I develop it in Kodak D76, diluted 1:1, and never have any problems with grain, even on 20 x 16in enlargements. When I come down to 35mm, I use Ilford FP4 or Kodak Plus-X.

In colour, I use Ektachrome 64 roll film. I avoid the faster Ektachrome emulsions unless the lighting conditions are really poor. For 35mm photography, I also use Ektachrome 64, which means I can standardise on one colour emulsion for everything. I know that some glamour magazines prefer Kodachrome 25 film, but I do not sell to these markets.

When the Mamiya M645 first came out, I fell for the advertising and switched to the 6 x 4.5cm format. However, I found this did not sell as well as 6 x 6cm format. Picture editors liked the larger format, because it lets them decide how to crop the image. They do not like photographers having the final say over how the rectangular picture should look.

Now, I use Hasselblad for roll-film shots, and Nikon for 35mm.

Planning a session

I think about photography twenty-four hours a day. I am always looking for ideas; they are running round in my head nearly all the time.

But I think you can sometimes over-plan a session. You need a lot of flexibility with a glamour shoot. The idea in your head may not suit the girl in front of the camera, and if the two are not compatible, you will never produce the picture.

I like to see the girl first, and then think of an idea that will work with her. However, occasionally these plans go wrong, and I find I am suddenly shooting something entirely different – and the whole session turns out to be a roaring success!

The warrior keeping guard over Julie's body is a defector from 'Star Wars.' He was originally spotted by Harvey Nielson promoting the film outside an ABC cinema and quickly snapped up for a photo session. Often, co-operation will cost no more than a few enlargements. After all, who is going to turn down the chance to pose with a pretty girl?

Flexibility is the main requirement. A good idea is essential, but you must be open to change, right up to the moment of shooting.

Most of my glamour sessions last about an hour. That is apart from the time it takes the model to change and put on make-up. During this hour, I will probably use about five rolls of 120 film – 60 shots.

I shoot up to two films where all the frames are almost identical. The pose remains the same while the smile changes, or the shoulder turns, or the hand moves. There is very little variety on each film.

After this, I may turn the pose around and shoot it from the other side. The individual frames are not important at the time of shooting. It is the idea which is important, and the way it develops.

One session contains just one idea. When the idea is finished, so is the session. I rarely go on to try other ideas at the same time.

This can appear expensive in terms of model fees, but look at it this way. For topless work, the average model fee is about £35 an hour, with a minimum booking of one-and-a-half hours. This works out to just over £50. For this, I produce sixty shots, including colour, with maybe four or five different poses based around one idea. The pictures then go to my agency, which sends them out to newspapers and magazines.

At the moment, the *Daily Star* pays £150 for their page 7 pictures. It is the same with the *Sun* – although they mostly use work from their own photographers. *The Scottish Daily Record* pays £90 for glamour shots. The colour transparencies bring in returns for a couple of years.

A session I recently completed has already made me around £250. On the other hand, some jobs fall completely flat. You just make no profit at all. One session seems to even out another. A quick return of £400 is followed by two sessions which cost you money.

I am probably earning a weekly wage which is fairly average. There is no great fortune to be made in glamour photography – unless I am doing it wrong!

The American Indian head-dress session is a good example of an idea which worked. I saw the head-dress as I passed a shop which had recently started stocking Western cowboy gear. One of my models, Julie James, was going to the States, so I thought this fitted in well for her. It was also coming up to Easter, and the head-dress made a very unusual Easter bonnet. And a little later would be 4 July – American Independence Day. This one colourful accessory had a lot of opportunities going for it.

I went in to the shop and borrowed the head-dress, leaving my bank cheque card and driving licence behind as security. Having my name in the local papers helped here, and the proprietor of the shop was only too pleased to lend the item to me.

Good accessories are normally difficult to obtain outside London. If a photographer on a national newspaper wants anything, one of the large department stores will send a lorry round with a selection for him to choose from. Out of town, it is not so easy. You have to convince the retailer that you are not going to run off with the goods, and that he will receive a credit when the pictures are published.

However, it is important to keep using different accessories – they help the photograph, and they help the caption.

At the moment, for example, I am shooting a series of pictures featuring an exercise bicycle. This idea came when one of my models said she was going to buy one. The photographs should sell well when the Milk Race is on, especially if the caption says that the girl is keen on cycling, and likes the exercise because it keeps her trim.

When I submit photographs, I give the girl's name, where she comes from, any unusual hobbies, and a few alternative caption ideas. Most of it is make-believe, but you can produce some amusing words from things the girl says. One model I worked with mentioned that she was helping her boyfriend to do some decorating – the caption said that she liked to go upstairs and get plastered!

Sometimes, a newspaper might be interested in buying just an idea from you. You can ring up the editor and suggest a theme for a week of pictures. A few of the national papers are very keen on this. Their own photographers will take the photographs, but you will receive a cheque for your contribution. I have earned £60 for one idea and £80 for another – and £30 for a suggestion that never worked!

Advice for amateurs

Freelance photography is just like any other job – you have to sit down and make plans. It is no use shooting unless you know what you are going to do with the photographs. You must have a market in mind.

Approach newspapers and magazines. Have a word with the editors. Find out if there is a need for the series of pictures you may be thinking of taking.

But do not concentrate on a single area. You could end up with too many eggs in one basket. A publication could close, or a new editor might bring in new ideas. If this was where most of your sales came from, you could be left out in the cold.

It is better to spread your work around, and this means getting a good agent behind you. Every sale that you can make, an agent might be able to repeat in ten different countries. Your fee might be only £20 a time, but that is a total of £200.

However, do not expect to see immediate returns. You need to have your photographs with an agency for at least a year before any cheques start arriving regularly. And in the meantime, you must keep working and sending in more photographs, or the fees will quickly dry up.

You need to be very dedicated to succeed at glamour photography. It is not an occupation where you can make easy money.

Is it possible to make a living from glamour photography?

I know one photographer who almost manages, but he is really geared up for the subject. He has a wide variety of props and backgrounds built in his house, plus a photogenic swimming pool! He is also full of ideas.

A photographer who only shoots the occasional glamour session at weekends can only hope to cover costs at first.

Try to get some photographs in print as soon as possible, even if it is only a local newspaper, and even if all you get is a by-line. Published pictures can bring in more work, though it may not always be more glamour photography.

I always weigh up the pros and cons of any job I am offered. In today's economic climate, any work is welcome. It is better to be out earning money than sitting at home waiting for the phone to ring.

On the glamour side, I probably shoot about three sessions a week. Then there are usually a couple of sessions a month where I use a girl in an advertising or product shot. The rest of the time, I am busy with other work – covering football matches, or pop concerts.

But no more weddings! I have a great respect for wedding photographers. It is a very difficult job to do Saturday in, Saturday out. I find it all too time consuming, though, and it does not stretch my imagination enough – although I have met one or two bridesmaids who made very good models!

No, apart from glamour photography, I prefer commercial work, mainly in the entertainments field. I photograph a lot of groups and solo artists.

All you have to do is look in your local newspapers, where you will find these people advertising their services. Contact them. Ask if they need any publicity photographs. Offer a good deal, and you will find that the word soon gets around.

However, do not make the mistake of underpricing your work. You will never make a living like that.

It helps to get an accountant behind you after the first year. In the meantime, keep receipts to cover all your main expenses, and write down details of all the fees you receive.

Every month, you should sit down and work out how much money you are making – or losing.

Before I went professional, I managed to look after my own accounts, as the profit I made was not very large. I declared it to the tax man, who made an assessment for the following year. If I did not reach this figure, I got some money back.

The tax people are easy to get along with if you are honest with them. Do not try to get away with anything – it is just not worth it.

Once you have a set of figures for your first year, though, I suggest that you take them along to a local accountant and ask for advice. Tax is a headache that a working photographer can do without.

Julie James is one of those girls who can make posing seem easy. But it isn't. If you are working with an inexperienced model, you will need to spend a lot of your time helping her to relax and pose naturally. It is often useful to have a scrapbook of glamour pictures, torn from magazines, which show a range of attractive poses. You can refer to these whenever you get to the stage in a photo session where you are stuck for ideas of how to pose the model next.

Six photographers/Colin Ramsay

In the early sixties, I was doing a lot of pictures of celebrities.

I would find out who was in the country to take part in a film, or attend a premiere. Then I would track them down and ask if I could take a few photographs. They could only say no – but most of the actresses said yes. It was good publicity for them.

Many of these pictures were taken in the London parks, but the public never seemed to recognise anyone. They probably thought I was just taking a few snapshots!

I used to do quite a lot of pop pictures at the time, too – the Beatles, and other groups. But these sessions were quite tiresome, because you were dealing with several people at once. Often, one of the group would be several hours late, so a shot that should have taken half-an-hour would need most of the day.

I preferred taking the glamour pictures.

In those days, the only glamour-type newspaper was *Reveille*, which had a huge circulation. This has folded now, of course. But it used a lot of pin-up pictures – girls in dresses and bikinis. Occasionally, the *Daily Express, Daily Sketch* or *News of the World* would use one or two glamour shots – but nothing topless.

There were a lot of film magazines at that time, like *Photoplay*, and these swallowed up many of my pictures of film stars and starlets.

I also sold to photographic magazines, like *Practical Photography*.

I did not have my own studio until some years later. Running a studio in the West End was – and is – an expensive business. Anyway, it was often difficult getting these people to a studio.

Most of the photography was done on location – in hotels, at their flats or out in the parks. And the easiest thing of all was to go down to the coast for some beach pictures. In the sixties, we seemed to have better summers!

If there was ever a situation which needed a studio, I used to hire one. However, there were not so many studios available for hire in those days, and you often had to provide your own equipment. Today, there are plenty of studios fully equipped with electronic flash, backgrounds and accessories. Then, you had to be self-sufficient.

I had several Mecablitz and Braun electronic flashguns. Using two or three of these together, I was able to produce attractive lighting, rather than just a direct flash effect.

I was using Rolleiflex cameras at first, and then a Mamiyaflex C2 and C3. Eventually, I switched to a Hasselblad.

I used 35mm film ocassionally, but most of my work was on roll film. Many of the situations required fast shooting, and I did not have to focus so accurately with the larger format – it was enlarged less to make a print.

I shot some colour in those days, but most of the pictures were taken in black-and-white. Quite a few publishers were still demanding 5x4in colour transparencies for reproduction. The trouble is that 5x4in cameras are very static, so you ended up with posed effects – there was no spontaneity in the pictures. And there was never time to shoot more than half-a-dozen pictures of anyone on 5x4in film.

At the start, all my work was speculative. I set up all the assignments myself, took the pictures, and then went out and sold them. I was developing a good market with pin-up magazines, newspapers and calendars. Then, as I became known, I started getting requests for specific shots to be used with editorial features. I also branched out into advertising – mostly shots which needed a pretty girl to promote the product.

Payments for these advertising pictures were far higher than for editorial work.

Snapping up girls

In the sixties, there were only a couple of London model agencies that had any girls good enough for glamour photography. These girls soon became well known, so you had to look around for yourself to find new faces.

Today, with well over twenty top agencies in London, there is still a shortage of the right sort of girl. There are plenty of girls available, but most of them are just not photogenic.

If you saw some of the 'page 3' girls without make-up and careful lighting, you would get quite a shock. Some of them are almost unphotographable. It is best they are kept in

black-and-white!

When it comes to finding new girls, the amateur photographer starts off with exactly the same opportunities as the professional.

If you look at the girls in the *Sun*, you will see that they come from all over the country. They have probably been working in some place like Brighton or Manchester for years and nobody has noticed. Then a photographer takes a series of good photographs and suddenly they are discovered.

It is simply a matter of putting the girl in the right environment and taking the right pictures – knowing what to do.

Of course, once a model starts to be successful, she moves to London, because that is where the work is, but most of them started from out of town.

How do you approach a new girl? Stealthily!

The biggest problem is gaining her confidence. It is no use going up and saying, "Right, I'd like to take some nude pictures of you." You will frighten the life out of the girl.

However, most girls with an attractive face and good figure will probably have an idea at the back of their mind that they could be an actress or a model. It is the glamour of show business which appeals to them.

If you say, "I think you are a very attractive girl and I would like to take some pictures of you," the girl will at least be flattered by your interest. If she says no, then no harm is done and you can walk away.

It is a good idea to show her some of your work – possibly some published pictures. Invite her over to your office or house to discuss the subject, or arrange to go and meet her parent or boy-friend.

Boy-friends, though, tend to be trouble. They say, "No, it's a very shady business." But

Opposite page

A fairly low camera angle helps to emphasise the model's long legs in this striking shot. The pose is unnatural — but it works.

This might look like a hay-loft, but it is not. The setting is an attic above the photographer's studio. The straw has been brought in for effect. It is often surprising how a fairly uninspiring area can be transformed into a good glamour location simply by the addition of a few accessories. Take a fresh look at a garage or cellar and see if they offer you any possibilities for photography.

parents are usually in favour of their daughter modelling – especially fathers.

Once you have found a new face it is advisable to shoot a couple of test films. A girl may look absolute perfection, but photograph badly. The first few photographs will show up any problems.

In most cases, the biggest problems with new girls are hair and make-up. They tend to get a bit slipshod about it. You have to educate them into thinking for photography.

Do not overdo the make-up – keep it simple and basic. The lips need a reasonable colour, while eye-shadow and mascara will enhance the eyes. A bit of blusher on the cheeks will give the cheek-bones a lift. Then lightly powder the face to eliminate any shines.

I usually start by shooting three-quarter length shots, with the girl standing up and sitting down. If she has a really attractive face, I will move in closer, but a lot of girls do not have the right looks for head shots, so you have to forget about these.

Whether we do any topless or nude pictures will depend on the girl. I am quite happy shooting a couple of rolls of film and taking it from there.

It is worth using both black-and-white and colour film for your test session. Some girls with very pale skin can look anaemic in colour, yet come over well in black-and-white.

Unfortunately, there is no camera filter you can use to make pale skin look healthier. If necessary, the girl will have to apply an all-over body tan.

Of course, if the girl is really keen on modelling, she will go and take a course of sunbed treatments to make her skin look brown and healthy.

The right equipment

When I first started out, I was equipped with just a Rolleiflex camera and a flashgun – yet I seemed able to tackle almost any assignment.

The market may be a bit more sophisticated these days, but a camera and flashgun is still all you need to make a start, providing you can add determination and enthusiasm.

Of course, you have to use the flashgun intelligently. It is no use leaving it fixed to the camera all the time. You must learn all about bounce flash, so that the one source of light illuminates both the subject and the background at the same time.

Once you have mastered the techniques, you can begin to think about selling your pictures.

As time goes by, you will start to build up quite a range of equipment. At first, though, it is best to save any spare cash for buying a better camera.

Good glamour pictures can be taken with inexpensive cameras, but there will come a time when you are not happy with the results. You will realise that the quality of your photographs is inferior to the quality of pictures reproduced in magazines.

If you are really serious about selling glamour pictures, then you have to start looking at the top equipment. A Hasselblad with a 150mm lens may cost well over £1000, but it will give the results required. It will also add to your determination, since you will have to try to justify the cost of the camera!

At the more modest end of the market, a twin-lens reflex camera is still worth considering. The problem of parallax makes composition a little more difficult, but this can be overcome with experience. Of course, now that Rollei have finished making twin-lens reflex cameras, you are left with just the Mamiyaflex and Yashica models.

There are always plenty of Rolleiflex cameras available secondhand, but you must look for one that is in mint condition – one that has been well-looked after and cared for. If you buy a Rolleiflex from a professional photographer, you will probably find that he has worn it out!

Still a good secondhand Rolleiflex could be better than a new 35mm camera, simply because of the larger format.

And then you have the problem of flash.

Braun and Metz are among the best portable flashguns. They are reliable and consistent.

Always buy the most powerful flashgun you can afford. When you use bounce flash, a

These variations on the theme of glamour photography show how a good photographer keeps coming up with ideas to make his pictures look different. Even the simple change of background colour is effective. All three shots were taken in the same studio — the luxurious-looking wall covering for the bath scene is simply a large rug. Notice how all the colours in each photograph co-ordinate. The pale pink of the bath sponge blends in with the skin tones — imagine the scene with a red or green sponge! The pink flowers of the hat match the pink material of the dress. The dark blue background helps to set off the pale blue dress. It is these small points which help to make glamour pictures successful. Pay attention to them.

lot of the light will be lost, so the more you start with, the better.

A lot of the smaller amateur flashguns are not powerful enough for professional use. They can be used for direct flash fill-in, but that is all.

It is worth investing in studio flash if you do a lot of indoor photography, but you will need at least two units for reasonable results. A single studio flash can give you a flash-on-camera effect if you do not use it properly.

There are several ways you can use two flash units. Most of the time, I position one on either side of the model, at angles of 45°. However, a carefully-placed white reflector can give you a fill-in light on the left-hand side of the girl if you are lighting from the right. Then you can use a second flash behind, to light the background or the hair.

It is well worth having a flash meter to determine the exposure.

Producing the pictures

It is possible to take good glamour pictures in a normal lounge, providing you can clear enough space. You will need a throw of ten to fifteen feet for full-length shots, but head shots can be done in almost any corner.

The main problem is setting up a roll of background paper. This is usually nine feet wide, but you can cut it down for easier handling in small spaces.

Of course, for some sessions, just the normal room furnishings might be adequate. Glamour sets for men's magazines mostly show simple backgrounds with the girl sitting in chairs and lying on rugs.

If you use your own house for photography, you can choose furnishings which will look good in glamour shots, and select venetian blinds and bamboo curtains that will make good backgrounds.

I plan each photo session carefully – not shot by shot, maybe, but certainly roll by roll. Experience is a great help in knowing what to take – it is not something you can learn in five minutes.

It obviously helps to study the market you are shooting for. If you want to sell 'page 3' pictures, go through several months of *Sun* and *Daily Star* newspapers to see what they are doing. (The offices of these newspapers will have back copies you can study).

If you want to shoot glamour with seasonal themes, make sure you know which magazines are likely to use your pictures, and whether they prefer colour or black-and-white.

Do you need to have a model release signed by the girl at the end of each photo session?

It is not essential. In a court of law, the fee you have paid the girl will be accepted as a form of contract. This means it is better to pay by cheque, rather than with cash, so that you have a record of the transaction.

However, it is advisable to have a release form signed, to forestall any problems. There was a case recently where a beauty queen resigned because glamour photographs she posed for appeared in a men's magazine. I am sure that she did not want them published, but if a model release form was signed, there was nothing she could do. Photographers could not afford to take pictures if there was a chance that the girl might try to prevent publication at a later date.

I do all my own black-and-white processing, developing Ilford FP4 and HP5 films in Paterson Aculux and printing on Kodak Bromide paper. I do not like resin-coated papers.

All my colour transparency film is sent out to a local laboratory.

The slides are mounted in card frames and I store these in plastic viewing sheets. Each sheet holds twelve photographs and enables a picture editor to see them all at once and make a decision.

Picture editors tend to throw the photographs about on desks and tables, so the plastic sheet also gives useful protection.

Black-and-white film is cut into individual negatives and each of these has its own storage bag. They fit nicely into small two-drawer filing cabinets with a sheet of card down the centre of each drawer.

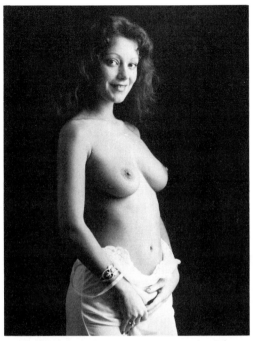

These shots of Annika were taken within a few minutes of each other. In a well-organised studio, it is possible to change the backgrounds as quickly as the model changes her clothes. This way, a lot of pictures can be taken in a short time. And that means more money from more sales!

A pretty girl in an expensive car—but you need not pay for either. This is the sort of shot you can take at motor shows. The high camera viewpoint cuts out the crowds of visitors, making your photographs look like studio pictures.

Unusual fashion accessories are always worth a few photographs. The selling period for the pictures might be short, but you can be sure of attracting the attention of picture editors for a few months. And if you file the shots away, there is always a chance that the accessories might make a comeback. In case you are wondering, these are space-age sunglasses.

My filing system is a bit haphazard, but it is based largely on the name of the model and the number of the frame. A booking out and booking in system tells me which magazines are holding my photographs at any time.

Going it alone

I do not use an agency for selling any of my work.

In this country, few of the agencies sell really hard. They just sit in an office waiting for people to ring up or call in. And for this they take 50% of the publication fees – an amount which I think is far too high.

If an agency can sell your photographs, then so can you. All you need is enough self-confidence to go round and see the publishers.

Although a lot of people will see you if you simply arrive at their office, it is best to phone and make an appointment first. You can explain what you have available, and they can say what they want to see.

A national newspaper, for example, always wants 20x16in glamour prints on double weight, glossy, unglazed paper. Most provincial papers will accept 10x8in prints.

Glamour magazines tend to like 35mm transparencies. They can load your pictures into a projector magazine, sit down, and see the whole set.

For covers, most magazines prefer 6x6cm transparencies. The format stands up well to enlargement and is easier to view and handle. Photographs for book covers and record covers usually need to be in this format, too.

There are around eighty record companies in Britain, but most of them are now commissioning the pictures for the covers. Even the straightforward glamour shots for some of the cheaper labels are being commissioned, although there is still a market here for stock material. If you have the right sort of picture, you can probably sell to them without too much trouble.

A lot of my sales are now overseas. I visit most countries from time to time.

In Germany, for example, in one city you may have a hundred or so different publishers. You cannot see them all in one visit, of course, but you can see quite a few over a period of two or three days. You do not need to speak German – they understand, and are pleased to see your work.

Locating the publishers is no problem. In Soho, or parts of Fleet Street, there are big racks of foreign magazines. It is easy to see which ones are using the type of material you shoot, and you can make a note of the names and addresses.

Or there are various directories you can find in libraries. These will often give a good idea of what is available.

It is important to keep doing this research all the time, because new magazines are published and old ones fold.

However, once you get to know a few publishers, they will probably let you know what they are doing, and even ask you to supply photographs for some of their new projects.

One problem with selling overseas is payment. The worst country for this is Italy. It is notorious for using photographs without sending out any publication fees. And they will ignore your letters or pretend they have not got your pictures.

It is difficult to go over there and complain, of course, especially if you do not speak the language.

In Britain, it is much easier to turn up on the doorstep of a publisher who owes you money. Fortunately, though, publishers in this country are not too bad about paying, although several companies I have had dealings with in the past have gone bankrupt!

Making a start

If you want to make a success of glamour photography, you must specialise.

I have seen photographers' cards which list industrial, commercial, wedding, insurance and glamour photography! But you cannot really arrive for work wearing a safety

helmet, industrial gloves, wellington boots and a bow tie. You must find the area which appeals to you most, and then concentrate on it. The going may be tough at first, but you will find your niche eventually.

It is no use going to a school of photography if your interest lies in glamour. You might learn a few useful techniques, but since most schools specialise in commercial and industrial work, much of your time will be wasted.

The only path for a glamour photographer is self-education. You must learn from all the mistakes you make as you shoot. Eventually, you should develop your own unique style, and this could make you very successful.

In the meantime, it is worth going along to courses run by other glamour photographers. You will see how they actually set up a session and take their pictures, and you may find out a little about their selling techniques.

Watching other people at work is a good way of learning a subject, especially if you also have the chance to take some of your own photographs under their guidance. Even if you make mistakes, at least you will have seen the right way of doing it.

Some courses run for several days, or even a week, letting you gain good experience for quite a modest fee.

Another thing you can do is buy a large scrapbook and use it to collect 'page 3' pictures, magazine covers, advertisements, and anything else which shows good glamour photography.

It never hurts to try to copy good photography – you can learn a lot by working out how the photographer produced the effects in the picture.

A good collection of glamour pictures can also provide you with ideas for your own photo sessions.

It is possible to build up a reputation as a freelance glamour photographer while doing a completely different full-time job. In fact, this is a sensible approach, because you will still have money coming in while you build up sets of pictures and make good contacts. However, it is going to take you several years to get anywhere.

But you will not become an overnight success even if you resign your present job and take up full-time glamour photography. It will still take years to shoot a useful stock of pictures and gain the confidence of publishers.

In Dundee, for example, there is a large publishing company which produces a newspaper called *Weekly News*. This uses glamour pictures – mostly of girls in dresses or bikinis. However, they rarely deal with photographers they do not know. First, you have to convince the paper that you have a good range of material they could use. And it is no use sending in photographs of just one girl. You have to submit at least half-a-dozen, because they like to make the final choice.

But it is a good market, and I wondered why they rarely used any photographs from local Scottish photographers. The answer, it turned out, was that few local photographers ever visited the paper, and the standard of work from those that did was not adequate.

In London, it can be quite difficult for a freelance photographer to sell pictures to a national newspaper. Many only accept work from members of the National Union of Journalists (NUJ).

But in the provinces, there are many newspapers which will use non-union material. They may not pay very much, but any work you can get published will help build up your portfolio and establish your reputation.

The low fees will mean that there is little competition from established professionals, and the newspapers will have a good reason for publishing your pictures if you photograph local girls.

You will need quite a bit of money in the bank if you do decide to turn professional. The problem is that you rarely get paid when a photograph is accepted by a publisher. Payment is usually on publication.

Most newspapers are quite good and pay within a month or so, but it can be several months, or more, before you see the money from some magazines.

If you have booked a girl from a London model agency at £30 or £40 an hour, and used quite a lot of colour film, you could find you have spent over £200 on a single session – and you will not see any return on this money for maybe six months or more.

However, one advantage of turning professional is that your work will improve more quickly. You will have to be absolutely certain that everything you shoot is saleable, and will show a profit on the time and money you invest in it.

Despite all the problems, it is still possible for a newcomer to make a success of glamour photography – if they have enough determination.

There is money to be made from speculative glamour shooting, providing the photographs are of the highest standard and show consistent quality. And once you have established yourself as a reliable photographer, commissions will begin to come from publishers who have used your work in the past.

Markets
& Models

The Mayfair Market
The Practical Approach
The Agency Operation
The Model's View

The Mayfair Market/Kenneth Bound

Mayfair is one of Britain's most successful men's magazines, with a circulation that has reached over 400,000 copies a month. It is also one of the most 'respectable' glamour magazines, being sold by newsagents who will not handle many of the competitive publications. The Mayfair formula is first-class fiction and features mixed with top quality photographs of attractive girls. Nearly all of the girl picture sets are from freelance contributors, so the magazine offers a good market for the glamour photographer. Unfortunately, few photographers seem able to produce the right material, as editor Kenneth Bound explains.

I have spent quite some time in Fleet Street, some of it with the *Daily Sketch*, some as Assistant Editor of *Woman's Own*. This means I have both a newspaper and a magazine background.

Brian Fisk, who actually founded *Mayfair*, was a working colleague of mine on the *Daily Sketch*. When he decided to set the magazine up with his wife, he asked me to edit it. I missed the first issue, which was done before I could join him, but I have been editor ever since.

Brian was tragically killed in a car crash in 1969, and so I have continued the magazine, along with Mrs. Fisk, from that time.

I have virtually grown up with the business, so to speak. I know quite a lot about what has happened over the years as far as this type of photography is concerned.

We often say here that the only time and place to judge a transparency is when it is on a light box. In other words, a photographer can say that he has got a marvellous idea and a beautiful model, but until you can actually see the transparencies, you cannot tell if it has worked, or if it has the quality.

But once on the light box, we can see at once if a transparency has that very special cachet which will really make a reader go back to that picture again and again.

On the practical side, wherever possible we prefer photographers to use Kodachrome stock, which we think gives better results than other films. We rarely use Ektachrome, and we rarely use colour prints. And never black-and-white, of course.

Now and again we will use roll-film transparencies, but because our entire origination process is geared to 35mm, we prefer not to receive the larger size if it can be avoided.

I do not think that a cheap 35mm camera produces good enough results – most of the photographers who shoot for us regularly are using either Nikon or Pentax. The transparencies must be absolutely pin-sharp, too, which means using a tripod. We never use soft-focus material.

And we must have a model release, of course, before we can consider buying a set.

Reproduction fees

For First British Rights – which means that the photographs go back to the photographer when we have finished with them, and he is free to sell elsewhere – the basic minimum fee is £200 for a four-page use of a set. We do not run under four pages on a set, and usually it is six.

We pay £600 for a set of pictures that goes in the centre and an extra £250 if we use one of the transparencies on the cover.

We may pay over the minimum rates, of course, especially if the model is a well-known actress, say, or a TV commercial model, or something similar.

Selecting the sets

There are probably the best part of 10,000 transparencies in the *Mayfair* offices. The majority of these will be sets which we have bought, but which have not been used. The remainder will be sets which have been submitted during the week.

We publish about 60 glamour transparencies in a typical month – the average girl feature has 10 transparencies, and we are probably using 6 sets.

In the course of a month, though, I suppose we receive at least a hundred sets of photographs – half of them from photographers we have never used before.

Unfortunately, hardly any of this material from new contributors is accepted – for clearly definable reasons.

There is absolutely nothing to prevent a set coming in the post and immediately commanding our highest price. There is no sales prevention. There is no, "Oh well, I can't pay him what I pay my best photographers."

If the photographs come in as a first-class set with everything right, then they are just as likely to be accepted and will go straight into the same money bracket as a set from a

These days, men's magazines use very few black-and-white photographs. A really good black-and-white set of a girl who has since become a famous singer or actress might be considered, but you should be shooting exclusively in colour if you hope to break into this area.

photographer we have used for years. But only if they have got what we need.

The problem is that photographers do not get it absolutely right for us.

We have to face the fact that many girls have good enough figures for successful glamour modelling, but a girl either has to have a very pretty face, or some other special type of attraction.

Sophia Loren, for example, is absolutely a classic beauty.

Brigette Bardot, on the other hand, is not, but she has that type of attraction which is first-class. Ursula Andress is another, in a different way – she looks imperious, but that type of look can come over extremely well.

So if the girl is at all plain-looking in the face, she needs to have some special factor of that sort. The problem can occasionally be overcome with beautiful hair-styling and beautiful make-up, but the first fall-down is usually that the girl's face is really not quite attractive enough.

The photographer must also remember that if the girl has an outstandingly good physical attribute, then the photo-set should show this to the best possible advantage. It can be a well-shaped bust, not necessarily large by any means; or prominent nipples, say; or a firmly-rounded bottom.

It would be a waste of time including this shot in a set for Mayfair — they do not use soft-focus pictures. You must study the market carefully before shooting so that you do not waste time and money on photographs which stand no chance of being published.

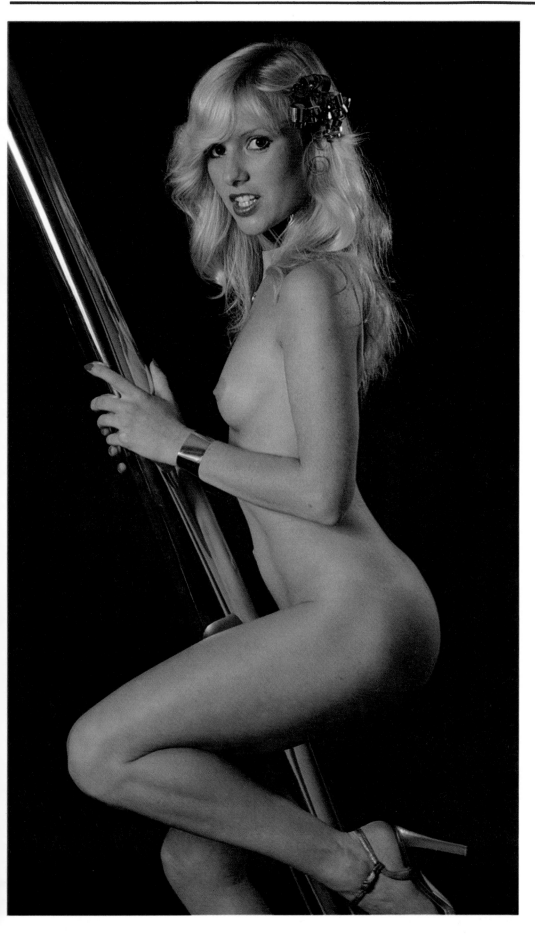

Do you know which of the men's magazines might be interested in using this type of studio shot? It is a question you must be able to answer if you are going to send them photographs. Since many magazines change their requirements from year to year, the only way to keep up-to-date is by studying copies every few months. This is called market research.

Against that, if the girl has one particular physical disadvantage, then the photographer should try to minimise this by means of pose and lighting.

Judging by the readers' comments we receive, the following types of model are very popular: girls who appear very young – though I am talking here of no younger than mid-teens; more mature women, late twenties or early thirties, say; girls with large busts; girls who have classically beautiful faces; and natural red-heads.

There are many, many reasons why photographs fail for us, but one above all others is posing. The photographer gets the girl to adopt old-fashioned 'Look at me boys' poses, and turns a perfectly normal girl into a 1943 American Army pin-up. It destroys the girl's personality and is definitely not for us.

Nor do we want the other extreme – the explicit open-leg shots. *Mayfair* has never gone in for this, so any set that is exclusively of this type is not likely to be accepted.

We are very keen on what we call 'progression of nudity.' This means starting a girl off fully clothed and then having her strip by degrees until she is fully nude.

Ordinary day-to-day clothes are fine for our purposes. We do not like a girl to look as if she was leaning against a Soho lamp-post ten minutes before the shot.

Underwear is an important part of any set. Again, no tarty overtones – keep it frilly and feminine. Many of our readers are keen on tight white semi-transparent knickers. The photographers often kit the girl out in a pair that are a size too small so that they appear as tight as possible.

Stockings and suspenders are still popular; so are fishnet stockings, French knickers, camiknickers and hooped socks. All in moderation, of course, and hardly all at the same time – though it has been known for people to try!

If a model lends herself to a particular outfit, make use of it – a young girl kitted out in school-girl clothes; an older woman in a waspie – whatever works best.

And the minimum of make-up. Over-applied warpaint tends to look cheap and nasty when it is photographed.

Most of these things a photographer can see by studying the sets that we use in the magazine.

The most important technical problem is that of flesh tones. They need to be a clean pinkish colour.

The worst transparencies are those which have traces of yellow or green in the flesh tones – when you reproduce them, the girl almost looks dead. And if the skin tones are too red, she will end up looking like a boiled lobster.

Generally, the printing process will exaggerate the faults, so a sallow flesh tone will look even sallower.

Each of our best photographers has his own technique – which he jealously guards – with lighting and filters to get those beautiful clean pinkish flesh tones.

It is no good a photographer looking at his set of transparencies and saying, "Well, it's not quite right, but it's not too bad, so I'll send it." He has to be rigorously disciplined with his standard.

This is undoubtedly true of focus and exposure. If the photographs are unsharp, or too dark, or too thin, then it is not worth our looking at them.

Advice to amateurs

There are a large number of photographers who hire a local model, or take photographs of their wife or girl-friend. This is the major source of our freelance contributions.

And it can be a marvellous source, because the wife or girl-friend has never modelled before, and so she is fresh on the scene. Also, there are some very good local models who have never thought it worth their while to see a London model agency, and so they have never been seen in a major magazine before.

The typical *Mayfair* photographer is not a jet-setting playboy figure. He is basically a first-class photographer – amateur or professional – who has a professional attitude to the way he tackles the problems and controls the shoot.

His technical ability is very high – but any amateur can achieve this if he is prepared to take the trouble.

If we see a promising set of transparencies from a photographer, we try to help him get over some of the problems. But it is not always easy, because they may be pictures of his girl-friend, say.

Now maybe she does not have quite the face for the set, but he cannot find anyone else he knows to photograph and is driven to using a professional model. And he may not be able to work with her so well. What you gain, you lose.

It is sometimes difficult getting photographers to the next stage. Often, they will give up, because it is an expensive business shooting rolls and rolls of film.

It's a pity, because we have helped several photographers to recognise what was inhibiting their sales, and they have been able to correct it.

But it is high time that photographers were leading us in this market – it has all been much the same for a number of years.

There are photographs that we can imagine which, if someone took them, I would buy at almost any price. You could imagine them, too.

Let me give you an example. Think of that marvellous poster of the girl in the tennis dress scratching her bottom. Now if somebody had said that he had this idea for a girl in a tennis dress scratching her bottom, everyone would have laughed. It seemed to have nothing going for it.

But what the photograph did show was supreme technical skill; the girl really looked as if she had only just thought of doing that and was not aware of anyone watching – a totally natural gesture tied to a lovely, almost innocent sexuality.

Any amateur could have got a girl in that pose and done it. She did not even need a pretty face. It was a cinch. Everybody was talking about it as the poster of 1980.

If that picture had come to me, I would have bought it immediately as a front cover for First British Rights of £500. Then I would have discussed what else could be done with it – calendars, posters and all the other rights that photographers negotiate and sell.

That transparency could be turned, in my view, into several thousand pounds. And any amateur could have done it.

The first thing he must do is think. Let us assume that he is photographing his girl-friend. Let him watch and analyse what she does that he might find sexy. He will often be surprised to discover that nudity has very little to do with this. It may be a certain look, or a certain pose.

The sexiest photograph that Clive McLean ever took was one of his own wife, and it was the opening shot of the set. She had a magnificent figure, but was wearing a long dress and sitting on a step with her legs quite naturally apart. The hem of her dress was just covering her knees, but you could see up her thigh to a pair of very tight white pants. It was the unconcious look about it that made the photograph successful.

The first thing a photographer must do is analyse what it is he is trying to capture. It is no good just asking a girl to take her clothes off. What is the pose he wants? What is the sexy moment?

If it happens to be the moment when a girl is taking a bath, then fine, shoot some like that. But think what it is that has the sex appeal before pressing the shutter release.

For example, you could find that it is very sexy when a girl is topless, but still has her pants on. Why not the reverse, where the girl is wearing a bra, but no pants?

These are the things that make you think, "Oh, that's good." But the thought must come first.

If a photographer turns his thoughts into half-a-dozen transparencies, then I can advise him what to do next to make them saleable to me. The pictures should range from almost totally clothed shots – perhaps even totally clothed – to one or two totally nude poses.

With a controlled shoot of just half-a-dozen ideas which the photographer thinks are sexy, I can react to both the ideas and the technical quality. He has to prove to me that he has the ability to 'see' a sexy situation. If he has that to start with, then we can soon guide him technically.

I firmly believe that photography can be learned far more easily than journalism. I think a photographer can be a top-flight successful photographer by learning how to

discipline himself, whereas writing probably needs more of a creative touch.

I am not saying that photography is not creative – it is highly creative. But what a photographer has to produce at the end is something that he actually sees with his eye. His eye is the camera. He has to make a mental click saying "that's sexy." Then he has to ask, "can I recreate that?".

If a photographer sends in a set of pictures which are technically marvellous, but we feel the girl is not quite right for *Mayfair,* then we could help him to find another model, probably near his home. And it would be a girl we felt was capable of getting into the magazine. This is a much shorter step than the photographer trying to find another model himself.

But there are very few girls who will not, under the right circumstances, make a successful set of photographs for *Mayfair.* That's because we are trying to find nice, normal girls.

Certainly, the photographer must not think, "no, that girl would not make it, her boobs are too small." The figure is not a great problem, because it does not matter to the reader. He does not demand that every girl has an hour-glass figure. We need the variety.

Shooting the sets

Few of the photographs we use are shot in studios with room settings. The majority are taken on location – and it is a common adage that it is harder to find the location than it is to find the girl.

One photographer, John Allum, does have a studio and has constructed – he used to be a builder – some walls and windows as a permanent feature. He moves different furniture in for each session, and most people wouldn't realise that the result is not from an ordinary location.

The location which does not work is what I would call the 'suburban' lounge. There is usually too much jazzy colour; too much dominating colour.

It has not got enough serenity in the background because there are too many ornaments and lamps; it all looks rather mixed up. I would rather use a plain studio than that.

If you want to use a suburban house, it is probably best to use a divan-style bed against a plain wall. You could get away with that, maybe even with a nice print on the wall.

Do not let any photographer think that if only he could afford to go to Greece, then he would get marvellous pictures. There are photographers living in Greece who send their pictures to us, so there is no advantage.

The outdoor location has some disadvantages. Often, the girl cannot relax because there is a possibility of being overlooked. She may 'freeze up' because she is scared of being seen.

Next, you can set up a shoot, but you cannot control the weather. In Britain, if it is overcast, then the flesh tones will go blue. On the other hand, a sunny day in a little woodland dell can be magnificent.

Outdoor locations are most useful for starting the girl off in her local village or home town – photographing her completely clothed against a landmark which local people will recognise. Or you can start the set off exactly where the average man first sees a pretty girl – in the street. That adds veracity, and is very good.

Outdoor nude pictures are more difficult, and depend not only on the weather. The photographer needs to find a location where the girl is not going to be suddenly surprised by a stranger.

Clive McLean once had a shoot where a guy had clearly cycled by, then crept about 400 yards through the undergrowth into a neighbouring bush. Clive went down one side of the bush to get another angle and walked straight into the chap, who then rushed off down the hill in his bicycle clips!

You have to be careful in other ways, too. Generally, there is no copyright of location. You can photograph a girl sitting on a bench outside a pub without any problems. But you would not do a photograph of a nude girl walking down someone's private drive without their permission, because it would imply that the girl had walked naked out of their home.

Many of the location scenes you see in glamour magazines are nothing of the sort. Rather than take cameras and lighting equipment into bedrooms, most photographers prefer to bring bedrooms into the studio. Here, they have much greater control over all the photographic aspects. It is not difficult to suggest a bedroom, or any other room in quite a small space. The girl fills most of the frame, so you only need to add a headboard, pillows and sheets to give the impression she is at home.

I would approach outdoor shooting the other way round. If you have got a pretty girl-friend and suddenly there is a fine day, then by all means go up to an obscure part of the Downs – but do not plan to do it until the day arrives.

If you have first got your sunshine, and the girl is feeling summery and warm, and the light is right, then you have more of a chance.

Presenting the pictures

It is useful for a photographer to concentrate on producing pictures to suit the style of one particular magazine.

However, I have often said to a photographer, "there is a lot going for this girl, a lot going for this set, but it is not right for *Mayfair.*" Then I have recommended another magazine which has, shall we say, a more down-market readership.

We consider ourselves at the top of the list, so I am only ever sending people down. I have never said that a set is too up-market.

So all is not lost if a photographer has not quite aimed it right. I know that other magazines have rejected sets that were not revealing enough for them and said, "try *Mayfair.*"

For us, the photographer must shoot a real girl so that her personality comes across. The amateur photographer has more chance with us, because we find it a positive factor for the girl to look like the 'girl-next-door.' Other magazines like to turn her into a sexual fantasy – we do it a little bit, but others do it all the time.

So yes, do aim for one magazine – preferably *Mayfair!* But all is not lost if your aim misses. We can and do suggest other magazines who are more likely to want that sort of material, even if they are rivals.

How many transparencies should you send?

We can tell nothing if there are less than 20 photographs. There have been several occasions where someone has sent in five reasonable transparencies and I have asked to see more. But the rest have been no good at all – he had picked the five best and there was nothing else.

The answer is to think in terms of around a hundred transparencies. It is not worth going to the trouble of asking a girl to co-operate in a set if you are not able to shoot at least that many. Also, three 36-exposure films give us a better chance to assess the ability of the photographer, and enough to select only the most flattering shots of the girl.

It also gives the photographer time to lead the girl through that 'progression of nudity.'

As soon as transparencies arrive at *Mayfair,* they are booked in. I see all the ones which arrive by post. If the photographer has phoned up and brought some in, then normally my chief sub-editor, Martin Burr, will take a provisional look.

Martin also sees photographers who call in out of the blue – but we usually find their stuff is hardly worth looking at.

If Martin finds a set he likes, without going so far as to say that we should buy the photographs, then he will bring it through to me and say something like, "the girl is great," or "the photographer's got something here," or, "the nude shots are no good, but there might be a cover among this lot." So it comes over to me at that stage.

When I have found a set of pictures I like, I will probably give it over to Martin, or maybe talk about it to other members of staff, but none of us working here are ever in any doubt about the top-class acceptances. There is no question of someone thinking a set is marvellous while someone else thinks it is terrible. If the photography and the girl are at the right level, then everybody who looks at them will say at once, "let's have 'em."

So you are not at the whim of an editor or an art director having had a bad day. We all know which are the pictures we want.

The photographs that are to appear in the magazine go through a very rigorous selection procedure. First, the transparencies are laid out on a light box and their number reduced to eighty.

At this stage, we eliminate any that are too revealing for us, and any where the girl has winked or blinked at the wrong moment. We also remove the badly-cropped ones, where the body is only half in the frame – that kind of thing.

Whatever the reasons, we always end up with what we consider to be the best eighty – because eighty is the number of transparencies which go into the magazine for our Carousel slide projector.

Although the initial selection may be done by one person, there are always two, sometimes more, seeing the projected pictures.

The first stage in reducing from eighty is reasonably simple. Certain pictures just do not have it when projected. They are competent, they are fine, but we know they are not going to last. Whereas the ones that are going to give that extra something begin to come out and hit you. And so we normally get it down to thirty.

Going from thirty to the ten or so we are likely to use is very difficult. In the end, you have to abandon things you would like to show, because otherwise you could not use any full-page pictures.

A photographer must not worry about this. If we have left out one of his best, it is only to prevent another of his very good ones appearing as the size of a postage stamp.

The rules of the last ten are that all parts of the body must be featured – face, boobs, legs, and so on. That often means that if there are five super leg pictures, four of them may have to go. But that is how rigorous the selection has to be.

Photographers and models

The type of material people expect us to consider for publication in *Mayfair* is surprising.

First of all, there is the pornographic material, of course. The worst example is usually a fairly obscene Polaroid shot – that is the absolute end as far as we are concerned.

The next stage is the amateur who has sent in colour prints – really no more than holiday snapshots.

The third stage is the photographer who has never mastered focus or exposure. His photographs are either fuzzy, too thin or too dense.

But it is not all a matter for despair. Most of the material is well worth the time spent considering it.

We prefer, though, that photographers post their pictures to us. It is very difficult to make a first assessment in front of the photographer – especially if he has brought the model with him! That often happens when the model is a girl-friend. It is highly embarrassing to tell a photographer that his girl-friend's figure or face is just not good enough. So sending by post is the best possible way.

I have made my fair share of mistakes, undoubtedly. The biggest and most common is not recognising a girl we have previously used under another name. This is particularly galling, because we always want to use true stories about the girls.

We have never, to my knowledge, turned down a super girl because she appeared no good to us. I have several times rejected sets from photographers who have later had other material published elsewhere, but that is usually because they did not come back to me with the new photographs.

Any clangers? Yes, I remember a very bad one. We once photographed a girl in a boatyard, on somebody's boat. The boat owner took us to the High Court because he said it implied that he had nudes on his boat. At the time, he was waiting for his membership to come up for the Royal Thames Yacht Club!

That was a lesson to us all. When you are using a location, check that it is either a public place, or that you have the owner's permission. Otherwise there can be untold problems.

Another piece of advice is never be surprised. I have learnt to say, "don't think it can't happen."

In my case, we were presented out of the blue with pictures of Lesley Anne Down in the nude, complete with signed model release. We just could not believe they were genuine – but they were.

Fortunately, we checked, and were able to use them. She was denying that she had ever done nude modelling, but she had posed for a boy-friend and he had got a model release signed.

    Do not ever believe it cannot happen. We discovered this when we wanted to find the Nudest Young Conservative. You do not believe that an attractive girl in the Young Conservatives will take her clothes off? You are wrong!

    What about some success stories to finish with?

If you are just starting to shoot for men's magazines, outdoor settings will probably give you the best chance of success. Both you and the girl will feel more at ease, and the locations may suggest ideas for shots. But best of all, this type of glamour photography in natural surroundings has one of the widest markets.

Roger Pearson is a photographer in Yorkshire. At the beginning, he was not very good technically, but got better, and developed his own style of shooting girls in situations. He produced a very successful girl set in an old train, and he did another good set of a girl in a pub with all the customers about. He improved his skills into making a very positive contribution to the magazine.

John Allum, too, was a great success story, where we co-operated together. He found that he could produce the most beautiful underwear shots, and made semi-nudity very sexy indeed.

Other than that, our successes have been with individual girls. We have spotted several girls who went on to make it in television and photographed them before they got there – Penny Irving, for example.

And there is a film of Caroline Dell that we still sell in the magazine through our film society. She was originally shot for *Mayfair* by her husband. He was an amateur photographer and the photographs were not technically perfect, but we used them. The response we got from readers was one of the biggest we have ever had in *Mayfair* magazine. And that was simply an amateur who shot pictures of his wife.

I would be delighted to look at the mail on my desk tomorrow morning, find a set of photographs, and immediately send a cheque for £1,000 to the photographer.

In other words, I can imagine a set of pictures well within the capabilities of a good technical photographer, allied to a good model, which has both sex appeal and freshness. The instant it arrived on my desk, I would want to make sure that we could forge a strong link with that photographer, so I would pay £1,000 straight away to show good faith.

I can imagine those pictures, so they must be capable of being taken. Really, it all comes back to the tennis girl poster.

And it shows – as far as we are concerned – that the market is wide open.

The Practical Approach/Robert Scott

Britain is the only country in the world with weekly magazines for amateur photographers. It also has one of the widest ranges of monthly photographic magazines.
All of these publications accept speculative material from freelance photographers. In fact, some of the magazines rely on contributions for their main features in each issue.
Market research has shown that over three-quarters of the readers of photographic magazines are male, so it is not surprising that glamour photographs are frequently used on covers and inside.
Practical Photography is Britain's best-selling monthly photographic magazine. Robert Scott, editor since 1976, looks at how glamour photographs play their part in selling the magazine.

It is not difficult to sell good glamour pictures to photographic magazines. All it needs is an understanding of this very specialised market.

The point that many contributors miss is that photographic magazines are not glamour magazines. Photographs of the local beauty queen are unlikely to be of interest, no matter how good the quality of the shots.

Readers of photographic magazines do not just want to look at photographs – they want to be told how to take similar shots.

If you are able to string words together into coherent sentences, and arrange these into flowing paragraphs, then you have a definite advantage over any photographer who thinks that a comma is a lens aberration and that a full stop is simply the difference between f/8 and f/11.

But literacy is less important than ideas. Fresh ideas are the life-blood of any magazine. Contributors who can offer a new approach to old subjects need never know what a rejection slip looks like.

Many freelance photographers ignore photographic magazines because the reproduction fees are fairly low. What they forget is that these magazines are quite happy to reproduce photographs which have been published elsewhere, providing there is a practical angle.

It is not necessary to shoot new material for photographic magazines. You can make new sales by creating features out of photographs taken during other assignments. You can even sell your mistakes as examples of photographic faults!

Finding features

Around one hundred contributions are sent to *Practical Photography* every month. Out of these, we probably retain two or three for possible publication. And most of these will be from regular contributors – photographers who have their work published in the magazine two or three times a year.

This is not favouritism on our part, but professionalism on theirs. These contributors have taken the time to study *Practical Photography.* They produce precisely the right type of feature for the magazine.

It is obvious that some would-be contributors have never seen a copy of *Practical Photography.* Why else would they send 'travelogue' features.

These contributions are usually along the lines of "Timbuctoo is a photographer's paradise," and end with the words "Good shooting!" In between is a description of the place, its mean annual rainfall, and why it is a good idea to avoid the water and the women.

Sometimes, the photographs accompanying the feature will be outstanding, but that does not stop it from receiving a rejection slip. That is because *Practical Photography* does not publish travelogue articles.

The photographer has wasted time and money submitting a piece which stands no chance of being accepted. Photographic magazines want features which explain how their readers can take better photographs.

How can this be applied to glamour photography?

In two ways. First, you can show readers how to take better glamour photographs. Second, you can use glamour photography to illustrate other photographic techniques. And both types of feature can be prepared quite easily while you are shooting glamour pictures for other markets. There is no need to set up special sessions for the shots.

Take a typical day's work. You want to put together some stock glamour pictures to send to a picture library. You book a model from a local agency and ask her to bring a range of clothes and accessories for outdoor glamour work.

You reach the first location around mid-day and take the first couple of rolls of film with the sun behind the girl, using electronic flash to fill-in the shadow areas. Then you move into the shade and fit a filter to overcome the blueness of the light from the cloudless sky.

At the second location, a few clouds have appeared and the light is bright, but diffuse – perfect for outdoor glamour photography. You shoot several more rolls of film, with the girl changing clothes two or three times.

Later in the afternoon, as the sun becomes lower in the sky, you shoot some moody sidelit pictures. Then, as the sun sets, you photograph the girl in the warm red glow of twilight.

When the transparencies are returned from processing, the results are excellent. You have a couple of hundred slides showing a wide variety of moods and settings, with the model in a range of different outfits. They are excellent stock shots, and should earn good money over the next few years.

However, before you post them all off to a library, take a look to see if there is anything which could earn money now from a photographic magazine.

In fact, the chances of putting a good technique feature together from stock shots is low – unless you planned for this by taking a few special pictures during your day's shooting.

For example, the first photographs of the day were taken by a combination of daylight and electronic flash. A good feature on fill-in flash is always of interest to photographic magazines – especially if it is illustrated with pictures of a pretty girl.

But photographs showing good use of fill-in flash give only half the story. You also need a few pictures taken at the same time without the flash. This will show the advantages of the technique.

After all, a good fill-in flash photograph rarely looks as if it has been taken with flash. Without a before-and-after comparison, your skill with the technique will not be apparent.

You can take this further by shooting a few frames with too much fill-in light. This will show how over-exposure spoils the natural effect.

These extra photographs take only a few minutes to shoot, and cost only the price of the film, but they can turn your initial glamour photographs into an excellent practical feature.

Another technique used early in the session was that of shooting in the shade. This is something you probably do not give a second thought – it is the obvious thing to do when the sunlight is bright and contrasty. But some amateur photographers still feel they need a bright sun behind their shoulders before it is worth taking a picture.

To prove this is wrong, you need two sets of pictures. The first must show the effects of taking portraits with the model facing into the sun – squinting eyes, heavy shadows and harsh highlights. These are the shots which you would not normally take, but which can be fitted into a few moments of a photo session if you have everything well planned.

The second set of pictures simply show the same girl, in much the same pose, but with the full tones and soft lighting obtained by shooting in the shade. And, of course, you take a few pictures before fitting a filter, to give another good before-and-after comparison.

If some amateur photographers are still shooting with the sun behind the camera, then many are also putting their cameras away when the sun begins to sink low in the sky. Glamour photographs taken in the twilight will be a new idea to quite a few readers of photographic magazines. Here you do not really need to take any pictures specially for the feature. Half-a-dozen striking evening photographs can be compared with a couple taken earlier in the afternoon.

A feature on evening glamour photography can describe some of the problems of shooting in these conditions. Did you need a tripod? Or a filter? Was a lens hood necessary to keep the low light rays off the lens? Which film do you recommend? How did you determine exposure?

Then there are the more general features which can be illustrated by some of the photographs taken during a glamour session.

A lot of photographers, for example, would like to book a model for a day, but do not know how to go about it. A simple article describing your own experiences would be a useful guide. How did you discover the model agencies in your area? How did you choose a girl from their directory? Was the agency happy to accept your booking, or did they require references? What were the model fees? Did you speak to the girl before the assignment? What sort of clothes and accessories did she bring?

This can be accompanied by a few pictures showing the girl in some of her different outfits.

Finally, do not overlook the point of the photo session. There is quite an art in taking 'stock shots' – photographs which will sell for year after year. The pictures need to be timeless, avoiding clothes and accessories which can be identified with any particular period.

This is a subject rarely covered by photographic magazines, yet all it needs is a few words and some striking examples of good stock photography.

These are just five ideas for features from one day's shooting. Of course, you would not use them all. No magazine editor wants to see the same girl illustrating a whole series of articles.

But if you plan pictures for a couple of technique features into each of the photo sessions, it will not be difficult to keep up a regular supply of well-illustrated articles to a number of different magazines.

Picture choice

Should you shoot in black-and-white or colour?

For the answer to this, you need to do a little market research. Buy a selection of different photographic magazines and count the number of editorial pages in each. Then count the number of these pages which are in colour. You will find that it is normally less than a quarter.

This means that – unlike glamour magazines – photographic publications will be happy to accept good black-and-white glamour photographs.

You have a choice. You can shoot everything in colour and hope that the magazine thinks your photographs are good enough to take up valuable colour pages. Or you can plan a glamour session completely around a photographic magazine feature and only use black-and-white film.

The sensible solution, though, is to use two cameras and shoot both colour and black-and-white. This gives you the widest possible selection of markets for selling your pictures.

It also means you can send both colour and black-and-white shots to the photographic magazine and leave them to make the final choice.

Of course, there are some techniques which can only be illustrated in colour. You cannot show the effects of a colour filter in black-and-white!

Colour pictures should be transparencies. Very few magazines accept colour prints, because prints do not usually give the best reproduction.

Most photographic magazines are happy to accept 35mm transparencies, and are not too concerned about the make of film used. Kodachrome certainly gives the best results, but Ektachrome is usually acceptable. Agfachrome is satisfactory if the photographs are not reproduced too large, but it can appear very grainy in full-page pictures.

However, if you can supply roll-film transparencies, then you will increase your chances of acceptance. Given a choice, any picture editor is going to go for the larger format.

In black-and-white, you should submit prints between 8x6in and 10x8in. Larger prints are not needed and can be a nuisance. *Practical Photography,* for example, keeps picture files in standard filing cabinets, and these will not accept prints over 10x8in!

Prints must be on glossy paper – textured surfaces do not reproduce as well.

These photographs were used to illustrate a Practical Photography *feature in August 1975. Under a title of 'Glamorise the girl-next-door,' the article gave simple advice on organising and shooting an outdoor glamour session. The pictures were specially shot for the feature.*

Photographs on glossy fibre-based papers do not have to be glazed, although this improves the appearance. Resin-coated materials are fine.

How many photographs should you send? The answer is about twice as many as the magazine is likely to use. This is where you need to take another look at the magazines you have bought. What is the average number of pages devoted to technique and glamour features? How many photographs are used in each feature?

Generally, you will find that features are about three or four pages long, with up to six photographs. This means that you should submit around a dozen shots. The picture editor needs a good choice, to make everything fit. Putting pages together is rather like completing a jigsaw – except that there is a choice of pieces to fill the spaces.

It is not uncommon for an illustration to be used because it happens to fit, rather than because it is the best example available.

Your magazine research also needs to note the type of glamour pictures used. How many topless shots appear? Are full-frontal nudes ever reproduced? This sort of information is essential. It is a waste of time illustrating a feature on fill-in flash with erotic nude pictures if the magazine is trying to sell to a family audience!

This sort of research is something you must do for yourself. You will not find the answers in this book, because the policy of a magazine can change from month to month. The publishers might decide to go for stronger glamour shots in an attempt to increase sales, or a new editor might disapprove of naked bodies and order a cover-up.

Writing the words

Once you have the photographs, it is time to think about the words.

You do not have to write a finished article to sell a feature to a magazine. If your photographs and ideas are good enough, a few detailed notes about each picture, plus a brief introduction may be enough. Most magazines have staff writers who can build a flowing feature around your photographs, providing they have sufficient basic information about how you shot them. These writers will have a 2000 word article with the printer before you have finished the first paragraph.

But if you can write an article around your photographs, do so. It will increase your chances of acceptance. It will also increase the publication fee.

Unfortunately, it is not easy to put a practical feature together. Descriptions of simple techniques can become long and confused unless you have a good grasp of the subject and can write clearly.

Here is the secret. Keep sentences short. They have more impact. They are easier to understand.

Avoid long words when several shorter ones are adequate. Write with brief paragraphs.

This does not mean that you are writing down to the reader. You are simply presenting information in a form which can be followed by someone without previous knowledge of the subject.

Most new writers make a serious mistake. They assume that their own knowledge of a subject is shared by the readers. This is not usually the case. A typical reader of a photographic magazine probably picks up a camera only once or twice a month, and thinks that using more than a dozen cassettes of film a year is extravagant.

This means that terms you take for granted may need to be explained in detail. You cannot simply say, "and it is a good idea to bracket exposures." You must expand this by writing, "and it is a good idea to bracket exposures – shooting frames at the next wider and smaller apertures to ensure that at least one is correctly exposed."

Of course, there is a limit to what you can explain. You cannot elaborate on every technical term, or a simple feature will soon become a complete manual of photography.

A lot depends on the magazine you are writing for. If it usually runs a lot of features for near-beginners, then your article must be set in very simple terms. If it is a magazine for enthusiasts, then you can assume a more knowledgeable readership.

As usual, it all comes down to market research. You must read several copies of the magazine you are writing for, so that you can produce material which comes close to their style.

Some magazines will print contributed features almost word for word. These days, though, it is more likely that someone will go through your text to make it conform to the style of the journal – the 'house style.' Depth of field may be changed to depth-of-field, for example, or f8 to f/8.

These changes are not real corrections, since both forms of the phrase or symbol are acceptable. In a well-produced publication, however, you will find that the same phrases and symbols are printed in the same form in different features. It is simple professionalism on the part of the editor and staff.

The magazine may also have a style of short sentences and paragraphs, so any writer who makes a habit of using 30 or 40 words between full stops could find that the feature has been repunctuated.

Some editors dislike the use of colloquial or slang words – 'umpteen' will be changed to 'many.' Some feel that English is more than adequate, and needs no help from Latin – so 'etc.' will become 'and so on,' while 'per' is struck out in favour of 'a.'

The style of writing numbers varies considerably. The *Practical Photography* house style dictates that numbers up to ten are written in words, while 11 and over appear as figures. However, there are plenty of exceptions when the number is a measure – "eight or ten people produced their 10x8in prints."

And two numbers written next to each other can be confusing, so a phrase such as "19 20-exposure films" will be written as "nineteen 20-exposure films."

That is why dates in *Practical Photography* are always written as "19 August 1981" and never "August 19 1981."

Fortunately, no magazine expects a freelance contributor to know all the subtle nuances of the house style. Providing you can supply a feature which is easy to read – and accurate – the editorial staff will knock it into the required shape to suit the particular publication.

Fees for features

If it is difficult to make a living as a glamour photographer, it is impossible to survive on the fees paid by photographic magazines!

You must look on these publications as providing a useful additional market, rather than your main source of income – jam for your bread-and-butter.

In the past, photographic magazines paid a mere pittance for a picture. They encouraged the view that having your photograph published was an honour, and that this was more important than the money.

Some amateur photographers went along with this, of course – and still do. They are the ones who do not have to use their fees for food.

These days, most publishers have come to accept that oft-quoted phrase, "if you pay peanuts, you get monkeys!" They are more prepared to pay reasonable fees to their freelance contributors.

You should certainly expect to receive around £10 for each photograph – more if it is used as a full page reproduction. There is a tendency to pay extra for colour, despite the fact that a black-and-white print costs more to produce than a transparency, and requires no less skill.

The professional rate for features is around £50 a thousand words, but you may have to accept a little less than this at first.

Some magazines pay for words and pictures by the published page. This is not always very fair, since the designer might have used several photographs quite small.

As an average, though, *Practical Photography* expects to pay between £30 and £40 for a contributed page – which means that a four-page feature can earn a photographer around £150.

Famous photographers can earn a lot more. One photographic magazine paid £800 for a portfolio of pictures during 1981!

Glamour with everything

Glamour sells. You only have to look at the massed covers of magazines in a newsagent to see how pretty faces and figures are being used to attract attention.

So as a glamour photographer, you are at an advantage when it comes to producing almost any kind of technique feature for photographic magazines.

As a glamour photographer, of course, you may not be very interested in producing technique features – but can you afford to pick and choose your assignments?

Photographic magazines get through a large number of practical features every month, and are always short of good material for future issues. If you can produce even half-a-dozen articles a year from your existing photo files, you will soon be able to buy that new camera!

Every time you carry out any kind of photographic operation, step back and see if it can form the basis of a feature.

Print retouching is an obvious example. You need to make two prints, both covered in dust and hairs. These prints, of course, are of an attractive girl. Then you need to show the various stages of retouching being carried out, and who better than a model to pose for these demonstration shots during a break in a glamour session? Make sure, though, that it is not the same girl who appears in the retouched print!

By adding these touches of glamour, your fairly ordinary article on print retouching suddenly becomes very attractive.

You can liven up other photographic features in the same way. Use glamour shots to illustrate the darkroom techniques of shading and dodging. Cut up prints of pretty girls to make a montage. Even a straightforward article on processing black-and-white film will look all the better if the photographs show a girl handling the tank and chemicals.

Feminists might not approve of this attitude, but it is simply a commercial approach, for a freelance photographer.

Covers and competitions

There are two areas where you can make money from photographic magazines without having to worry about words to go with the pictures – covers and competitions.

Every magazine needs a cover picture – and you will find that most use a glamour photograph most of the time. But it is no use simply sending off a batch of your best slides and waiting for the cheques to roll in. You need to match your photographs very carefully to the different magazines. This means more market research.

Some magazines, for example, aim to link the front cover picture with one of the inside features. Where possible they will use one of the photographs submitted for the feature as a cover shot. Sometimes, though, the photographs may not have the right sort of impact needed for the cover, so a shot will be selected from a colour library.

This means that there is little opportunity for freelance photographers to submit cover pictures. It is unlikely that just the right shot will arrive at just the right time.

Other magazines, though, use cover shots which have little or no connection with the contents. Here, you can submit single photographs for possible publication.

You still need to be very selective. Take a look at recent covers of the magazines and see what type of glamour pictures are preferred. Are closely-cropped head-shots being used most of the time? Does the magazine go for sexy poses on the cover, or does it rely on the simple beauty of the girl to attract attention?

You can assume that the type of picture you see on a cover is the type of picture that magazine wants to see from contributors. Most editors try to aim for a continuity in covers. They want readers to recognise the magazine from a distance each month. So although the colours and photographs may change, the overall effect will usually be much the same.

Competitions offer you more scope to be creative.

You might wonder whether competitions are worth entering. The answer is a definite yes. First, a competition presents you with a precise brief – it is a good discipline to work to the requirements of someone else. Second, the photographs you shoot can still be sold to publishers or sent to libraries, just like your other work. Third, you might win!

Most photographic magazines run regular competitions where glamour pictures can be entered. The *Practical Photography* 'Photo Girl' contest is a good example.

Prizes are usually photographic equipment. Many distributors are willing to donate equipment in return for the publicity given by a contest. This means that the magazine does not have to spend very much when running a competition.

However, even if you are not interested in the equipment on offer, it is still worth entering. Most photographic dealers will give you a good price for unused, boxed cameras or accessories. You would probably be able to negotiate an even better price for a part-exchange deal.

A lot of photographers waste their time entering competitions. Their photographs stand no chance of winning, simply because the rules have been ignored.

The first rule for entering a competition is to read the competition rules.

You might find, for example, that you are not eligible to enter, because you are not an 'amateur' photographer. There is no hard-and-fast definition of an 'amateur.' When asked, *Practical Photography* usually says that it refers to someone who earns less than half of their income from photography.

Even this definition has caused queries. One person wrote to the magazine saying that he worked in a colour processing laboratory – did this disqualify him from entering photographic competitions? No, it did not. The definition was amended to read 'someone who earns less than half their income from taking photographs.' It is as good a definition as any, but check the rules to make sure no other criteria are being used.

Check the other rules carefully, too. If colour transparencies are asked for, do not send colour prints – yes, it happens! And if colour prints are acceptable, you will nearly always find that glossy paper is required. Do not enter on textured paper – your prints will not make it to the short list.

Check that you are sending the right size of photographs, and the right number. If only one picture is required, do not send more. If up to three photographs can be entered, why reduce your chances of winning by sending less?

Then read every word written around the competition, to pick up the clues about what the judges will be looking for.

The *Practical Photography* Photo Girl contest, for example, usually suggests that the girl should be photographed in different clothes against different locations. It adds that at least one head-shot and one three-quarter length picture would help to show different aspects of the model.

Despite this advice, there are always entries which show the girl in the same clothes, in the same location, with almost identical poses. The girl would have to be very good, and the quality of the shots superb, for the entry to be considered even for the short list.

It will help to look at a few recent issues of the magazine and study the type of glamour pictures used. If 'arty' shots are rare, then you would do best to avoid this style in your entry. Be creative, be original – but keep within the style of the publication.

Finally, never give up. You have little to lose and everything to gain by entering every glamour contest you can find. One day, the judges may be attracted by your model and your style of photography.

Post your pictures

Photographic magazines offer the widest possible scope to anyone starting glamour photography. You can make money from single shots with covers and competitions. You can sell features on glamour photography. You can increase the chances of acceptance for other articles.

Are you good enough to teach other people about glamour photography? If your work is accepted for publication, then the answer is yes. The standard of photography – and glamour photography in particular – among most amateurs is very low. Anyone who can sell glamour shots is much better than average.

All you have to do is study the market carefully, put your words and pictures in an envelope, and post them off to the editor.

The Agency Operation/Chris Matthews

A picture agency is the middleman between photographer and publisher. Photographers submit their pictures to the agency, which then markets them to clients. For this, the agency takes a commission — usually around 50% of the fee paid for the photographs.

An agency frees photographers from all the problems of selling pictures, leaving them more time to take more photographs.

A good agency will also have many more contacts than a photographer, which should mean more sales, both in Britain and abroad.

One of London's best-known colour libraries is Spectrum. Spectrum specialises in variety. Their stock list covers more than 100 different subjects, from 'abstracts' to 'zoos.'

Chris Matthews, Manager of Spectrum, describes how the library operates.

We like to have photographs of everything at Spectrum. We do a lot of business with people who need many different subjects. Someone working on three or four separate jobs will be able to find all the pictures they need in our files.

We have strong areas and weak areas, of course, and areas we do not touch at all. But we have a reputation for handling a broader range of subjects than almost any other library in town.

Right in the middle of the stock subject list are girls, roughly divided into head-and-shoulders, romantic, bikini and nude.

As I see it, the market for stock glamour photographs falls into two groups. First, there is the sexy type for calendars and magazines. Second, there are the softer, more delicate images used for advertising.

The girl in a stock glamour picture must be a professional model. If she is not professional, she will not look professional, and she will not look right.

The girl-next-door is no good, even if she has a fantastic face and a fantastic body. Without experience, she is going to look uneasy when she gets in front of the camera.

Clothes and jewellery must also be considered carefully. This is a stock business – we are not after a single quick sale. I want to keep selling a shot, so anything that can date the picture must be avoided.

Up-to-date fashion is no use. We might sell it for a few months, but then it is finished. T-shirt and jeans are better – they never go out of fashion. But sometimes jeans have flares, and sometimes the legs are tight – so do not show the full length. Crop the pictures at the knees.

As a rule, steer clear of jewellery that can date a photograph. Pearls and diamonds are in fashion one moment, and out the next. If you want to use accessories, keep them simple, not flashy. Use a plain silver band, or something similar.

Choosing a format

Large format is always better than small format. Roll film is preferred for most glamour photographs.

This is probably because many of our clients stand over a light-box all day and it is rather difficult to see a 35mm frame unaided. They cannot be bothered to get down with an eyeglass to look at every picture. It is much easier to see a 6x6cm or 6x7cm transparency.

Spectrum does not discriminate against the recently-revived 6x4.5cm format, but we are not getting as many people using it as I expected. We have around 2,000 photographers on our books, but only two or three of them shoot on 6x4.5cm all the time.

If it is the right subject, a good 35mm transparency will get into the files, and it does not matter what film is used. But 35mm is up against competition. If we have similar photographs on 35mm and 6x7cm, the larger transparency stands a better chance of being used, sometimes even if the smaller slide is slightly superior.

We have an office wall covered with pages from magazines which have used Spectrum pictures. I think three of them are from 35mm originals. The rest are from roll film.

Presenting your pictures

How should you approach a picture library – in person, or by post?

Just turning up on the doorstep is not acceptable. You should always phone first. Describe the sort of photographs you take, the market you aim at, and the format you use. Then ask if the library would be interested in looking at what you have.

If you do not live too far away, you may be given an appointment to meet one of the library staff. Otherwise, you will have to put your pictures in the post.

But I would rather meet the photographer personally than find a packet of 950 transparencies on my desk in the morning.

Either way, though, the phone call is essential. If your type of work is something the agency has plenty of, a few minutes conversation can save everyone a lot of wasted time.

For safety's sake, it is best to present transparencies individually. Never use glass mounts for slides – cardboard or plastic mounts are adequate. And make sure your name and address is on every single mount. If there is not enough room for the full address, just a telephone number will do.

It is not so important to mount roll-film transparencies. They usually come back from processing well-protected in plastic sleeving. You can just cut the sleeving and the slides together into individual frames. But you must still add a label with your name and address to each slide.

There is no need to mount slides into expensive card frames – most libraries will remount the photographs they retain.

We have our own particular way of mounting at Spectrum. Once the mount has been taken apart, there is no way it can be put together again. This way, we can tell when a client has removed a transparency from its mount.

Do not place transparencies in translucent paper negative sleeves or bags. It is not possible to see the picture through this material. If a photographer sends us 500 of these, it makes editing his work a very laborious process.

Making a living

Spectrum have around 2,000 photographers on their books. Out of these, only around 20 are full-time professionals. The remainder are amateurs.

But the word is misleading. These photographers are only 'amateurs' in the dictionary definition. Their work is of a professional standard. It is simply taken by people who do not make their living from photography. Airline pilots, for example, or coach tour leaders, or archaeologists – people who travel all over the world in their work.

I do not know of anyone who makes a living simply by selling photographs through stock picture libraries. Whether I know anyone who could is a different matter. Some of the top professionals probably could if they had their work in the right places and got the right sort of deals. But they do not. They accept commissioned work, or write books.

I know one or two people who come close to making a living out of stock photography, but I do not think it is really a full-time occupation. You would have to select two or three libraries with completely different requirements. You would have to work to tight briefs given to you by these libraries, and just take these photographs all the time. You would need a large capital investment to last five years while you built up a healthy stock of pictures in each area. And if it was raining over here, you would have to go abroad to keep shooting.

If we are talking specifically about glamour, then I would say there is no way that you can make a living simply by taking glamour pictures for stock. At best, once you have a good selection of photographs with a good agency, you might earn enough for a well-deserved holiday each year.

Supplying the stock

It is not worth rushing round to a picture library if you have half-a-dozen super shots from your last photo session. Spectrum wants to see a minimum of 300 photographs before they will even consider taking you on. We do not like dealing with two rolls of this and one roll of that. Apart from anything else, it does not give the photographer much of a chance of making sales.

If you came along with just three really good glamour shots, they would go into a filing drawer with hundreds of others. And if they get put at the back, they could lie there for a long time. A client will start at the front and go through until he finds what he wants. Then he stops. He may not reach the back, so he does not see the three latest shots.

You need to get yourself strongly represented in just a few subject categories. It is no use supplying one picture of the Eiffel Tower, one of the Taj Mahal, one of a nude girl and one of a cat. If you specialise in pictures of Egypt and the agency sells six shots of Egypt, you want three of them to be yours.

It is the same with glamour. If you specialise in outdoor glamour and the agency sell twelve outdoor glamour pictures for a calendar, you want some of your work among them.

Keeping new work coming in all the time is just as important. On the other hand, we do not like a photographer to be too heavily represented in one section. Clients like to see a broad band of different styles and ideas within each category.

A good photographer adds something of himself to his work. You can recognise it without seeing his name. Clients do not want to see the same sort of thing over and over again. We do not want clients knowing what to expect. We want them to come to Spectrum because we have a wide range of photographs in our files.

A photographer may ring up and tell us about a great girl he has found. He describes what she looks like and says that he is thinking of shooting this, this and this. We may tell him to concentrate on the first two ideas and forget the third, because he did something similar last year and the shots have not started to sell yet.

There needs to be this communication between photographer and agency. We talk to them and they talk to us.

Terms for transparencies

Saying goodbye to your top transparencies is something you will have to get used to if you want to work with an agency. Like most libraries, Spectrum are not interested unless you will part with your work for a minimum of five years.

We have to reserve the right, though, to return the photographs at any time. A set of slides which has been sitting in the files for a couple of years without any sales might be sent back.

According to our contract, the photographer does not have the right to reclaim the pictures before the five years are up. We are fairly flexible, though. I do not think we have ever refused to return a few slides if the photographer has found a market for them himself. We do not work like that.

On the other hand, if a client is holding one of these transparencies for future use, then we would not ask for them back. The five-year clause protects us in these cases.

The transparencies are not returned automatically at the end of the five-year period. They stay in the library until the photographer wants them back, or until we decide that we cannot sell them any more. That can be ten years later, or more.

I am very happy when I find a photograph still selling after fifteen years, because it must be a really good shot. It must be what stock photography is all about.

Unfortunately, not all transparencies will survive for fifteen years. Parts of the emulsion can fade, giving a colour cast to the image. Fortunately, that is not a major problem for Spectrum. We have material in our files which dates back to before the library started over eleven years ago.

Keeping track of thousands of transparencies is not as difficult as it may seem. Everything is coded and cross-referenced.

For example, the start of the reference code on a transparency might tell me it is a picture shot in Japan. I can go to the Japan file, look up the number and find a description of the photograph. I can find out where it was taken, and the name of the photographer. The card will tell me when the slide came into the library, and give a history of any sales.

A separate index contains details of all the photographers and lists the reference number of each of their photographs in the library. If a photographer wants his work back, we can soon locate all the categories under which he is filed.

We are not too keen, though, on photographers who keep phoning up to see if their pictures are selling. We are happier when the photographer views his work as a long term investment – forgotten about until the money starts to come in.

Some agencies build their name on the work of certain photographers, and that is fine, because it suits the market they are going for. But it does not work for us. We sell photographs, not photographers.

A publisher does not care that we have great pictures of dogs by Jim Sproggs – he just wants great pictures of dogs.

I could not tell you how well any particular photographer is doing at any time. If there are any sales, he will get a cheque.

Payment for pictures

Like most libraries, Spectrum pay photographers 50% of the fee each time one of the pictures is used. We keep the other 50% to cover the running of the library.

It can be six months or more, though, before the photographer receives any money. A lot of companies are using stock picture libraries at the moment because money is tight. It is cheaper than commissioning work. But because money is tight, companies are slow in paying their bills. Chasing money is becoming more of a problem.

It would be optimistic to think that all invoices sent out in January will be paid by March. I would hope that they would be cleared by May. After that, we would start to apply pressure for payment. But we only mail payments to photographers once every quarter, so it would be June before the cheques were sent out.

Sometimes, the photographer will receive money before a picture is published. That is because some book publishers accept invoices when the sale is made, long before the book actually appears. But an invoice is always sent out before a picture appears in print.

Except, of course, when the library does not know that a photograph has been used. Usually, a batch of slides go out to a client, some are retained and the remainder come back with the official order. Occasionally, though, the client will forget, or hang on to a photograph which does not appear on the order.

There can sometimes be a problem with travel companies, too. They use a lot of stock material in holiday brochures, and often reprint pictures from one year to the next. These reprints come from film separations used the previous year – they do not need the original transparency again. But a new fee is due to the library and the photographer.

Some of the more organised travel companies know well enough when they are repeating pictures like this. They phone up and say that they want to re-use the separations from the 1976 brochure. That is fine – we will invoice them. But some companies do not let us know. We have systems for checking, but there is no foolproof method.

We rely to some extent on the photographers. We never mind hearing from someone about a photograph that has been seen in a magazine or book. The chances are that the invoice will already be out, but it pays to be certain.

Shooting to success

Spectrum is a general picture library. We hold files of glamour shots, but we do not specialise in this category. We cannot accept unlimited quantities of glamour transparencies.

However, if anyone has the time, money, experience and skill to go out and hire a top model for some quality photographs in a first-class studio or good location, then we are interested.

But you are probably talking about £300 a day for the model, and this is just not viable for most photographers shooting stock photographs.

This might sound discouraging, but there are agencies around that do well out of glamour sales. Photographers must shop around until they find a library that likes their style of work and deals with the right sort of markets.

A photographer making a couple of thousand pounds a year with Spectrum might see his income drop to a few hundred pounds at another agency – and vice versa. Picture libraries are like any other sort of retail outlet – you can't buy buttons on a whelk stand!

The Model's View/Pat Keeling

Pat Keeling has been a successful photographic model for several years, travelling widely in Britain and abroad on assignments. Recently, she formed a partnership to run the Pat Keeling Model Agency, which has its offices in Leicester.

I started modelling by taking a course at a local school. And I have to admit that I would not have known anything about the business, or how to conduct myself as a professional model, without this course. It gave me an insight into what it is all about.

I learnt about make-up, hair, manicure, diet, exercise and deportment, as well as photographic and fashion modelling. These are the basics that any model must know. But I also discovered that a model's life is all auditions!

This means that you need a good portfolio of photographs and your own index card. You need to be on a model agency's head sheet, and in a model directory – anything that

can publicise your name and face.

You also need to visit photographers and advertising agencies with your photographs so that they can get to know you.

These are the sort of things that you learn from a course. I do not think that any girl can suddenly say, "I am going to be a model," and get it together right away. She would be too inexperienced.

It is possible for an amateur photographer to take good pictures of a girl who has not modelled before if they have a good relationship – if they feel at ease together.

Often, a photographer will meet a girl and ask her to model, and she will be very nervous for the first few sessions. This shows in the pictures. It is only after several sessions, when she knows the photographer better, that the photographs will start to improve.

A professional model, on the other hand, is not nervous at all. She can turn on the charm and the looks for the first photograph of the first session. That is the difference.

If a photographer is trying to make a living out of the pictures, then using a professional model has got to pay off. In an hour, it is possible to shoot some really good pictures without a lot of hard work. The girl just turns it all on for the photographer.

When I have a photo session with a photographer, I like to feel at home. It is nice to have a friendly atmosphere, so you are completely at ease. Then you can give your best and make sure the pictures are good.

One of the worst things any photographer can do is make the girl feel that he is looking at her from a personal point of view, rather than purely photographic. That is very off-putting and will make many models nervous.

A top model can cast the feeling aside, but it will put other girls on edge and they will not be able to give their best.

One of the worst incidents that happened to me was before I started the agency. I was booked on an assignment in Worcester. It turned out that the photographer was a complete lunatic – he wanted pictures of me gagged and bound!

He rented a room above a shop as a studio. I discovered that the only reason he got this was so that the shopkeeper could come up and watch! It was a nightmare, a complete nightmare.

As soon as I got out of the place, I drove back to Leicester at top speed. However, the next time I was in Worcester, I called in at a police station. I should have done this after the assignment, but I was so nervous, I just wanted to get home.

The police, apparently, knew all about my photographer – he had left the country with £2,000 worth of camera equipment on hire!

You are dealing with many different personalities in this business, and a good model will try to get along with them all. But it is not always easy.

I remember a trip to South Wales for some beach shots with a photographer who might be called 'eccentric.'

He drove his car like a maniac, accelerating and then jamming on the brakes all the time. I had to ask him to stop the car so I could get out and be sick, because my stomach was shaken up so much from the car ride.

He was the sort of person who would suddenly go off in a trance, in a complete world of his own, when he would not hear anything you said to him. I had to watch for these moments and let him collect his thoughts until he was down to earth again.

The main asset of a good model is to understand these people and recognise the type of person they want you to be. If possible, you go along with it.

Booking a model

I prefer photo sessions to be in a photographic studio, or on location, but we do accept some bookings for photographers' homes. It depends on whether we know the people.

We have quite a few amateur photographers come to our model school 'passing-out' shows, and they often ask if they can book a girl for a photo session at their own house. If we have dealt with the photographer before, and the girl is happy to go along, then we do not mind at all.

But if new photographers come along, we like to check them out before we send a girl. A phone call is not enough from someone you do not know. We like to meet a photographer and have a chat – learn a little about them.

Amateur photographers are often a member of a photographic society, so we can usually obtain references. These are the sort of positive steps we take to look after the models.

And with any new client, we make sure the money is paid before the assignment. This is no deterrent to a genuine amateur photographer, but it will put off anyone else.

Being in Leicester, our rates are a little cheaper than London. Semi-nude photography with an experienced model is around £20 for an hour, £60 for a half-day and £100 for the day. Full nude is around £25 an hour, £75 a half-day and £125 for a full day. These rates are reduced if the girl has only just completed a course.

These fees give the photographer full copyright of all the pictures. We do not mind the girls signing model release forms, if required.

Starting the session

I think it is really nice if the model is looked after on an assignment. I like being offered coffee when I arrive, and something to eat at lunchtime.

I always recommend that models take along a small snack on a full day assignment, because they never know what the situation will be. Some photographers will keep you working all the time, and there is nothing worse than feeling hungry and trying to put on your best performance when you have a rumbling stomach. It is much better to have a break, relax, and then get back to work.

I also like to know what the assignment is all about a few days beforehand. Then I can go out and buy any extra accessories which might be needed – this is a professional approach.

If the photographer's brief is very precise, then it can help to see any pictures or sketches that he is working to. This makes it easier to adopt the correct pose. But most jobs are much better if you can just flow from one pose to another.

A lot depends, though, on the photographer. Some amateurs always seem to be doing things wrong with the camera or the lighting. There is always a series of mistakes which slows everything down. This can get very boring, although you try not to show it.

With a professional photographer, on the other hand, there is usually a rapport which builds up as the session progresses. The photographer follows the poses of the model, shooting as the poses change.

Professionals, too, are usually more open to different ideas. Some amateurs build up a way of working which gives good results and they are then afraid to introduce any changes. This is not encouraging for the model.

An amateur photographer working with an amateur model is at a big disadvantage. He will have to direct her all the time, which means that the girl is not contributing very much to the session, and the photographer is only repeating what he has done before.

A professional model working with an amateur photographer can add plenty of ideas from her own experience.

This has happened with a photographer I know. He first approached me at a bus stop, before I was a model. I was very apprehensive about agreeing to a photo session, but he put me completely at ease.

Over the years, he has continued to photograph me. However, now that I am on the professional circuit, I am in touch with all the latest ideas and I can pass these on to him. They may be techniques he has never tried before, but he is willing to experiment. From these experiments, we have come up with some terrific photographs.

The ideal situation is to have a long chat with the model several days beforehand, to turn over ideas. When the photo session starts, the photographer should have everything ready so that it all runs smoothly.

If an amateur photographer books a professional model, he must try to aim for a professional standard himself.

The Model's View/Yvonne Wake

A lot of amateur photographers take glamour pictures because they like photography, and they like photographing girls. Shooting the picture is the main attraction.

If one or two of the photographs can be sold, then that is a bonus. For most amateurs, glamour photography is just a hobby.

Some may have a dream of becoming successful, but this rarely happens. There is not the market for the sort of work they produce. And there are too many good photographers around already established.

Most of my modelling has been for amateur photographers. I started with weekend courses for *Practical Photography,* and then did photo sessions for some of the people I met.

I have been to one or two camera clubs, but this sort of work does not appeal to me very much. They all expect topless modelling, but none of the photographers seem to know what they are doing.

I have no idea how many pictures have been published. So many different people have taken photographs that there is no way of keeping track. I know that I have appeared in several different photographic magazines, and some photographers have won competitions with the pictures they have taken.

The ideas man

Amateur photographers never seem to plan a photo session. They rely on me to come up with the ideas.

Modelling is boring when the photographer is simply copying other people's pictures. You cannot put any life into poses when you are asked to pout, and put your finger in

Yvonne Wake was introduced to modelling by an amateur photographer. He entered her in the Practical Photography *Photo Girl contest — and she won. Since then, she has undertaken many assignments for the magazine, including work at the last two* Olympia Photo World *exhibitions. She has also modelled for Club Olympus, several camera clubs, and many other photographers.*

your mouth, and just do the one-hundred-and-one things you have done one-hundred-and-one times before.

Modelling is much more fun when the photographer has put some thought into the photo session and come up with a few attractive ideas. Of course, this cannot happen until he has handled a few sessions first.

There is one photographer who has photographed me several times now. At first, he was terribly nervous. He did not know what to do. But now he comes along to a photo session well prepared, and his photographs have improved dramatically.

He is now more concerned about shooting one or two good photographs, rather than taking as many pictures as possible in three hours.

I always like to talk to the photographer a couple of days before the photo session, so that I know what is expected of me. It helps me sort out the clothes and accessories I need to take along, and lets me known how I should arrange my hair.

Also, if the photographer is paying for a studio, as well as my time, it seems a waste of his money if you have to spend a quarter-of-an-hour talking things over at the start of the photo session.

However, I prefer not to meet the photographer, unless it is essential. If he is going to photograph me a couple of days later, I have to turn up looking good – and make-up takes quite a long time! I would rather speak on the phone.

Usually, this is no problem. Most of my bookings are from photographers who have seen me modelling elsewhere, or have seen my picture in a magazine. They know what I look like.

I always make it very clear from the start – before we talk about money – that I will not do nude photography. Fortunately, this does not seem to have affected the amount of work I get.

Model management

I like to get on with the photography as soon as possible. It is nice to have a quick cup of coffee when you arrive at the studio, but I do not like wasting a lot of time chatting about nothing. I have other things I would rather be doing.

It is good, though, when the photographer allows plenty of time for me to change and arrange my make-up.

Changing facilities are never very good. I have given up expecting much. Privacy and a mirror is all I ask for. Hot running water and good lighting is a bonus.

I do not really mind how long the photo session lasts. I am used to modelling for hours on end. A lot depends on how well the session is going. If the photographer runs out of ideas very quickly, then it can be difficult to keep posing for even an hour. But if everything is running smoothly, I can keep going for six or seven hours, as long as there is a break every now and then.

With outdoor work, it is nice to go out for the whole day, just stopping occasionally for a drink and something to eat.

Of course, it can be very difficult for a photographer to plan a long photo session shot by shot. And anyway, this can be rather restricting. Spontaneous poses are often much better than those based on other photographs.

Really, the photographer needs to have a clear idea of what he wants, but should be ready to follow up anything new which presents itself during the session.

Often, I find that people do not have much idea of what they want until I start to do something they do not like. And then they know exactly what they want!

The clothes I am wearing help me with posing. Shawls and see-through tops are popular with photographers. It is the way you wear them which is important – not the clothes themselves.

Since I do not model full-time, I have quite a limited wardrobe, and I have to come up with new ways of wearing the same items.

I try to take along quite a few changes of clothes to a photo session, even though I know that I will end up wearing only two or three. Photographers are never very specific about what they want you to bring, so you have to give them a good selection.

Also, you never know what colour the background will be, so it is essential to have a few similar items in different colours.

Although some of the clothes I use for modelling are everyday wear, I also try to buy a few items specially for photo sessions. I have a swimsuit which I would not dare wear on a beach!

Human approach

Some photographers assume that girls who model are not very intelligent. You pick this up quickly from the way they talk down to you.

Perhaps it is true that some girls are not very bright – but this goes for some photographers, too! Many models, in fact, are well-educated, with views and opinions of their own.

Of course, it is not a good idea to start talking about politics or the economy during a photo session! However, a few photographers would obtain better pictures if they started treating models as equal partners, rather than as servants.

Almost as bad are photographers who put you on a pedestal and treat you like Dresden china.

I think I have improved quite a lot during the two or three years I have been modelling. At first, my smiles looked forced; now I can make them appear natural. And working with different photographers means that I can pass on ideas from one to another.

When I first started modelling for inexperienced amateurs, the photographs were not very good. The quality of the pictures depends on the experience of both the girl and the photographer.

A good model can make a valuable contribution to the planning and shooting of a photo session. She is not just a pretty face!

Techniques

Multi-images
Filters
Make-up
Portrait lighting
Black-and-white and colour
Mixed lighting
Backgrounds
Keep shooting
Dual markets

If you do your own processing and printing, do not overlook the opportunities for special effects. The demand may be more limited than for straight glamour shots, but there are also far fewer photographers producing this type of work. There are two distinct markets for special effect photographs. Most profitable is the commercial and advertising side. Here, though, much of the work is commissioned. You will only receive assignments once you have become known.

One way to get pictures published is by submitting them to photographic magazines. They love photographs which demonstrate interesting techniques. And if the effects include a pretty girl, your chances of a sale are almost certain. There is useful money waiting for anyone who can produce these pictures, and then describe in detail how they are done.

The pictures on these pages first appeared as part of an article on 'Fun Photography' in Practical Photography, December 1976.

'La Ronde' (top) showed how an existing image (left) could be transformed into an attractive design. The full step-by-step details explained how the multiple image was produced by rotating a sheet of enlarging paper on the baseboard and giving repeat exposures. Readers were shown how to divide the number of images into the degrees of a circle, and how to rotate the paper by this amount between each exposure.

'Strip-tease' (far left) showed how multiple exposures could be made in a roll-film camera, using a sheet of tracing paper in the waist-level finder to plot the position of each successive image. The print is from a single negative.

There are hundreds of different filters fighting for a place on the front of your lens, but only a few of them are likely to improve your glamour photographs.

Most useful are the soft-focus filters. These take the hard edge off images and are often added to hide a model's skin imperfections. However, soft-focus can also give a more romantic atmosphere to photographs.

Diffraction filters scatter light from the bright areas of the image, while holding most of the detail in the mid-tone and dark areas. These filters are especially useful when the subject is back-lit.

For a stronger effect, try a pastel filter. This gives overall softening to both detail and colour. It is especially suitable for head-and-shoulders shots (opposite top).

Also useful — when used in moderation — is the 'spot' filter. This gives a photograph which is sharp and clear in the centre, but with a strong soft-focus effect round the edges (opposite bottom).

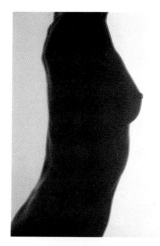

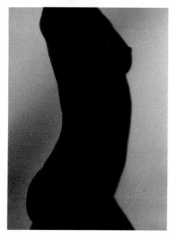

Few girls can afford a permanent sun-tan. Their skin may look brown and healthy for a month or two after an overseas holiday, but it will probably be paler for the rest of the year.

You can bring back the healthy look by using a filter. Unfortunately, there is no one filter which will work for every photographer. A lot depends on your choice of colour film and the colour temperature of the lights you use. Experiment to see which filter suits you best. It will almost certainly be one of the following — 81A, 81B, 81C, 85, 85B or 85C. The 85 series gives the strongest effect. An 81EF filter is also very good, but is not available in all filter ranges.

The photographs above show the effect of adding a warm-up filter to the camera lens (top, without filter; below, with an 85B filter).

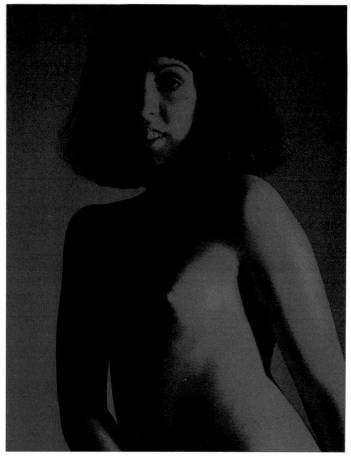

Filters need not be restricted to lenses. You can use them over lights, too.
The photograph on the opposite page shows the result of splitting an orange and a yellow filter over a light aimed at a roll of grey background paper. With a small selection of filters, you can produce a whole range of colour effects from the one roll.
On this page, you can see what happens when coloured lights are aimed at the model.

When you take glamour photographs, you probably leave make-up entirely to the girl. This is fine if she is an experienced model. But new models may not know what is needed. This means that you must tell them. These pictures show some of the basic steps.

For sharp, clear results, it is essential to start without any make-up on the face. Ask the girl to use a cleansing lotion, and follow this with a toner. Next, she should smooth in a little moisturiser to protect the skin.

Small skin blemishes or slight darkness under the eyes can be hidden by blending a little erase over the area. Then the complete face and neck should be covered with foundation. A small damp sponge can be used to smooth this over the skin for an even

tone. Check that the eyelids and lips have been covered and make sure that the foundation has been taken down well into the neck line. Nothing looks worse than a face and neck of different colours!

Mascara helps more than anything else to bring the eyes alive. It separates and accentuates the lashes, making the eyes seem larger and wider. Check that the girl has not splashed the colour as it was applied. She should use

it first on the upper lashes, and then on the lower, being careful not to smudge the make-up as it dries. A lot of time should be taken over the eyes — they are the main feature of many photographs.

Adding the cheek blusher is an important step in shaping the face. It should follow the curve of the cheeks when the model is smiling. Placed high along the cheekbone, it will lengthen the face. Placed on the roundness of the cheeks, it

will broaden the face. Ask the girl to sweep the colour upwards and outwards. She should then soften the edges by blending the blusher into the foundation base with her fingertips.

Next, the entire face and neck should be powdered. This forms a solid base for the rest of the make-up. A cotton wool pad can be used to pat the powder on gently, then sweep it lightly to remove the excess and leave a smooth finish. Framing the eyes with pencil will start to shape the face. The colour should be smoothed in lightly to accentuate the curve of the brow. Heavy lines must not be used — they will dominate the picture.

The shape and colour of the eyes is brought out by eye shadow. Here, blue is being used in the crease line. The same colour has also been applied under the outside corner and blended in to remove the hard edges. Next, a paler blue will be added to the eyelids and the area immediately under the eyebrow. Each new application must be blended in with the existing make-up to avoid any harsh outlines.

The shape of the nose can be altered with make-up. A dark foundation over the whole area will make it appear smaller in photographs. Dark foundation just at the tip will make it seem shorter. A broad nose can be made narrower by applying dark foundation down the sides. A short nose can be made longer by applying a pale foundation just at the tip. A flat nose can be given more shape by applying pale foundation down the whole length.

Lipstick is best applied with a brush — this gives a cleaner line. The girl should start with the lower lip, drawing the outline and then filling in the colour. It will be easier if she starts from the outside corner and works towards the centre. The shape of the lips can be altered by careful use of the brush. They can be filled out, or any unevenness eliminated. Lip gloss should be used for extra shine. This wears off, so the girl should keep it handy during the photo session.

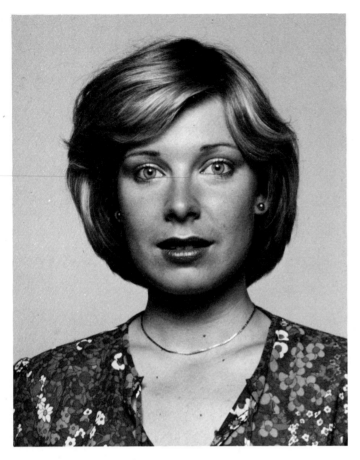

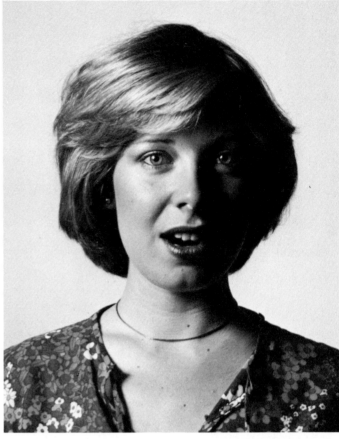

You will probably find that most of your lighting for glamour photography stays much the same from one photo session to the next. But you need to know how to alter your basic set-up, when necessary, for different effects.

This is not a manual of lighting techniques. If your knowledge of lighting is limited, buy one of the several good books on this subject that are already available. Check your need for further knowledge by seeing if you can say how many lights were used for each of these four photographs. Where were the lights positioned?

Above: a single light, used close to the camera.

Top right: a single light used to the left of the camera. This set-up normally needs a reflector at the side of the model to throw light into the shadows on the face.

Bottom right: one light close to the camera, plus a second light positioned behind the head and aimed at the hair for the 'halo' effect.

Opposite page: a single light, placed behind the model and to one side. A good lens hood is needed to stop this light shining directly on the front element.

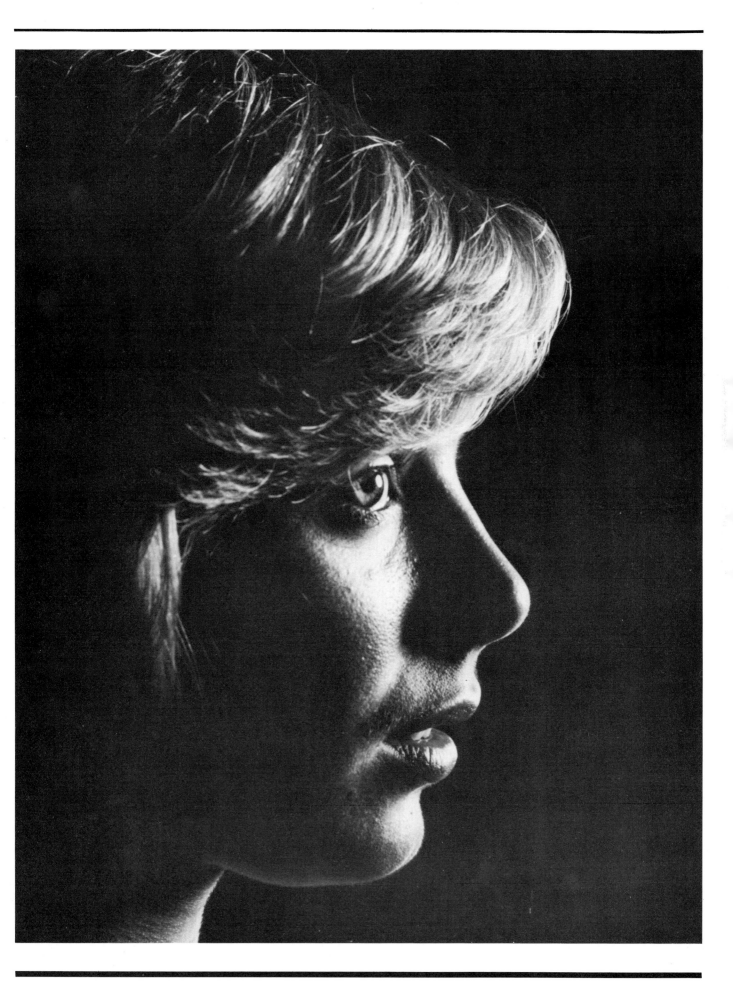

When shooting stock pictures, you will make more sales by having both black-and-white and colour photographs available. This gives you the widest range of possible markets.

The only way to duplicate your photographs is by using both black-and-white and colour films during the photo session. Do not try to produce black-and-white prints from your best colour shots at a later date — the quality of the prints will never be as good as when you print from original negatives.

Using flash in daylight is a technique you must master. Most outdoor glamour shots are taken with the sun behind the girl. This avoids harsh shadows on the face. But it can also put the face in the shade. A weak light from a flash fixed to the camera is all that is needed to bring back the detail (opposite page).

With a computer flashgun, the required amount of 'fill-in' light is often provided simply by setting the switches as if you were taking a picture indoors. But run some test shots to see if a little more light, or a little less, gives better results.

Most cameras must be used at a shutter speed of 1/60 sec for flash exposures. This means the model must keep fairly still, or you will see two images on the film — one from the flash exposure, another from the daylight exposure. The black-and-white picture on the right shows an extreme example of this. In fact, this shot was taken with a camera which allowed flash to be used at any slow shutter speed. The exposure time for this picture was 1/15 sec. The results, in fact, need not be unattractive and you will see the technique used from time to time by different photographers.

The subject of a glamour photograph is the girl. Backgrounds should be kept simple and discreet.

One of the most common backgrounds is the seamless roll of paper, available in nearly 30 different colours. This is usually supported on a frame or stand above the girl, with the paper running down to the floor. But it is just as effective to lay the roll on the floor and fasten the loose end to the wall.

There is no need to run the paper out along the floor for most shots, since you will rarely photograph the full length of the girl.

However, although paper is an excellent background, you need a little variety from time to time. Keep your eyes open for any fabric, screens, blinds and panels which might be useful.

The photographs on these pages offer a few ideas to start you off.

You have probably read about photographers who shoot thousands of frames of film to produce just twelve pictures for a calendar. This might sound extravagant, but they know what they are doing. When you photograph a good professional model, she will change her pose slightly after each exposure. Many of the poses will be good — a few will be very good. While you are shooting, it is impossible to say which pictures are working. The expression might be wrong in one, a hand badly placed in another. All you can do is keep shooting. The more film you expose, the better your chances of some really good photographs.

As a matter of routine, many professional photographers shoot off at least one complete roll of twelve exposures on each set-up.

The photographer shooting
these pairs of pictures was
looking for the widest
possible sales. In each case he
has taken one discreet pose in
addition to the topless shots.
This means that photographs
from each session will sell to
those magazines which
accept topless pictures, and
those that do not.
It is worth following this
example whenever you are
shooting stock pictures for the
glamour market.

Reference

Men's magazines
Photographic magazines
Calendar publishers
Picture libraries
Models and model agencies
Studios
Processing laboratories
Studio flash
Studio accessories
Presentation packs
Useful organisations

Reference Section

Men's magazines

Club International

Paul Raymond Publications Ltd, 2 Archer Street, London W1V 7HE.

Club International is a sophisticated men's magazine, in the *Playboy* tradition, and quite similar to stablemate *Men Only.* Only top quality colour material is required, and 35mm Kodachrome is the preferred format. *Club International* follows the usual quality men's magazine format, publishing a series of pictures of each girl, together with a story about her. However, the editor says that freelances stand the best chance of success with truly original work: 'don't just duplicate what you see in the magazine – the chances are you won't be able to do it as well as we can. Go for something original and spectacular!' Fees range from £500-£1,000, but are usually towards the top end of this scale.

Escort

Paul Raymond Publications Ltd, 2 Archer Street, London W1V 7HE.

This Paul Raymond Publication is somewhat down-market of *Club International,* and is more 'reader-orientated.' The type of girl featured in this magazine tends to have a less glamorous image than those pictured in the other Raymond Publications, and is more of the 'girl-next-door' type. A difference between *Escort* and other leading magazines is the use of very short glamour sets of 3-4 pictures to form double-page spreads. Photographers who have good glamour material in smaller quantities than the 100 or so transparencies required for a basic submission to other publications, may therefore find *Escort* a useful outlet. Some eight sets of this kind are used each month. Single pictures are required for the front cover, back cover and centre spread. As with all leading glamour magazines, transparencies must be of excellent quality and 35mm Kodachrome is most favoured. £200 is paid for two-page glamour sets.

Fiesta

Galaxy Publications Ltd, Hermit Place, 252 Belsize Road, London NW6 4BT.

Fiesta describes itself as a 'down-to-earth men's magazine that is also read by women.' It uses colour sets of exceptionally pretty girls, preferably those who look 'real' rather than 'modelly,' and who have not been seen in other publications. Submissions should consist of at least 100 transparencies, and should preferably have been shot on 35mm Kodachrome, though 6 x 6cm transparencies are also acceptable. £300 is paid per published glamour set.

Knave

Galaxy Publications Ltd, Hermit Place, 252 Belsize Road, London NW6 4BT.

Knave is aimed at a more sophisticated market than its stablemate *Fiesta.* Only top quality colour sets of very attractive models are required. Much of the published glamour material is bought from freelances submitting on a speculative basis, so *Knave* are always pleased to hear from would-be contributors who can produce the required quality. Glamour sets normally run from 7-11 pages, with the pictures showing the model in a variety of positions of varying 'strengths.' It is important to include some shots in each set that could be used on the cover. In this case, the pose should be erotic, but the model should be partially covered so that the magazine can be safely displayed in newsagents, and there should be no sign of nipples or pubic hair. As with *Fiesta,* a minimum of 100 transparencies is required per submission, and 35mm Kodachrome is required. *Knave* pays £500 per published set, plus £50 if a cover shot is used.

Mayfair

Fisk Publishing Co Ltd, 95a Chancery Lane, London WC2A 1DZ.

Mayfair is another quality men's magazine using a high percentage of freelance material. In fact, nearly all the photographs and major features are the work of freelance contributors. Required are colour glamour sets taken in up-market surroundings. The editor says: 'Much care and thought must go into the production of a glamour set, particularly the semi-nude photographs and the erotic use of clothing.' Backgrounds should be real-life locations, such as a nicely furnished flat, but little outdoor material is used. The magazine is also particularly interested in seeing pictures for possible cover use. The cover always features a girl, who should be sexy, provocative, natural and head-turning. She must not be totally nude, and nipples must not be shown. An occasional touch of humour in a cover shot is allowable. The subject should be shot as a square composition, but allowing a further quarter-depth above this for the magazine logo. The background should be reasonably plain and not variable, so that a logo can either be projected or reversed out. A lot of thought should be given to the erotic use of clothing and suggestion of sex appeal or sexual situation, together with a fairly simple colour scheme. The editor adds: 'Get your focus and flesh tones right before thinking of submitting. If these two factors are not right, nothing will work.' 35mm transparencies are preferred. 6 x 6cm material is only used if the subject is of outstanding interest. Fees for glamour sets range from £200 to £600, with £150 upwards paid for covers.

Men Only

Paul Raymond Publication Ltd, 2 Archer Street, London W1V 7HE.

Men Only, which has undergone some considerable changes in recent years, was first established in 1935 by City Magazines Ltd. Some years ago it was taken over by millionaire strip club and theatre owner Paul Raymond, and now claims the highest UK circulation of any men's magazine. Like the other quality men's magazines, each glamour feature consists of a series of shots together with a short biography of the girl featured. Pictures should portray beautiful girls in quality locations. Men Only attempts to maintain a highly contemporary image, so photographers intending to produce material for this market should pay close attention to trends and fashion in clothing, make-up and settings. Single pictures for use in illustrating articles and stories are also needed, but for this purpose the photographer should show a really original and creative approach. A really well-photographed picture of a girl dressed erotically is more likely to be used in this context than a nude. If contemplating this type of submission, contributors must study the magazine with great care in the first instance. As usual the

preferred format is 35mm Kodachrome. £500–£1,000 is paid for published glamour sets.

Penthouse

Penthouse Publications Ltd, 2 Bramber Road, London W14 9PB.

Penthouse is described as a sophisticated men's magazine appealing to a readership mainly between the ages of 18 and 30. The magazine uses top quality glamour sets featuring very beautiful girls. Freelances are advised to submit a few sample shots in the first instance, to see if the editor would be interested in a full-scale series of the particular girl. Preferred format is again 35mm Kodachrome, although 6 x 6cm material is acceptable. Sets normally run to between 6 and 10 pages, for which £75 per published page is the basic minimum rate.

Health and Efficiency

Peenhill Ltd, 3 Hallgate, London SE3 9SG.

Although not a glamour or men's interest magazine, Health and Efficiency does have picture requirements that bring it close to the other publications listed here from a freelance point of view. This publication is, of course, entirely concerned with naturist/nudist subjects. It cannot be emphasised too strongly that this is not a market for 'girlie' pictures of the type used by glamour magazines. Potential contributors must study the magazine carefully before submitting, and ensure that they do not submit unsuitable material. Outdoor pictures of people in the nude are required. Pretty young women are the preferred subject, but men and groups are also welcome. The

emphasis is on healthy outdoor activity. Photo-features, consisting of a series of pictures accompanied by a short story about the people and location involved, stand a much better chance of acceptance than single pictures, though these are also used. Both black and white and colour photographs are required, and in the case of colour any size of transparency from 35mm upwards is acceptable. £20 per page is paid for colour material, and £10 per page for black and white.

Other magazines

The larger newsagent chains handle very few glamour magazines. W. H. Smith, for example, only display Mayfair at many of their branches. However, a little investigation of independent newsagents and street vendors will reveal a bewildering array of publications with arousing titles.

Titles appear and disappear every year. Some of the magazines are published by back-street operations whose only interest is to make a 'fast buck.' They are often little concerned about the quality of the pictures they publish – and even less concerned about paying for them!

If you come across an unfamiliar title which you feel might offer a market for your pictures, write to the editor first, asking for details of publication fees and conditions. The style of the reply – if any – might give some clue to the efficiency of the organisation. Check that a telephone number is given. If possible, deliver your work by hand, so that you can gain some impression of the size of the organisation.

Photographic magazines

Amateur Photographer

IPC Specialist and Professional Press Ltd, Surrey House, 1 Throwley Way, Sutton, Surrey SM1 4QQ; telephone 01-643 8040. Weekly.
Aimed at photographers of all levels. Uses single cover shots, as well as features on glamour photography. Features up to 1500 words preferred. Fees by negotiation.

Camera

EMAP National Publications Ltd, Bushfield House, Orton Centre, Peterborough PE2 0UW; telephone 0733 237111. Monthly.
Described as 'a quality publication showing the best in contemporary amateur photography.' Scope for creative glamour photographs showing the use of interesting or unusual photographic techniques. Cover picture normally linked to an inside feature. Fees from £25 a published page.

Creative Photography

Carlton Communications Ltd, 10 East Road, London N1 6AJ; telephone 01-253 4628. Monthly.
Creative Photography takes much of its material from the Swiss-published German-language magazine *Photographie.* All the colour reproductions are from the Swiss original, which means there is little scope for speculative contributions to the UK publishers.

Photography (incorporating Photo Technique)

Model and Allied Publications Ltd, 13-35 Bridge Street, Hemel Hempstead, Hertfordshire HP1 1EE;

telephone 0442 41221. Monthly.
A 'how-to-do-it' magazine aimed at the photographer who has reasonable photographic knowledge and wants to learn more about pictures and equipment. Cover picture normally linked to an inside feature. Features between 900 and 1400 words preferred. Fees by negotiation.

Practical Photography

EMAP National Publications Ltd, Bushfield House, Orton Centre, Peterborough PE2 0UW; telephone 0733 237111. Monthly.
A magazine aimed at everyone who wants to take better photographs. Publishes features on glamour photography, and also uses glamour pictures in colour and black-and-white to illustrate photographic techniques. Accepts black-and-white photographs for picture files. Fees from £8 for pictures and from £20 for each 1000 words published. 'Notes for contributors' available on receipt of a stamped addressed envelope.

SLR Camera

Haymarket Publishing Ltd, 38-42 Hampton Road, Teddington, Middlesex TW11 0JE; telephone 01-977 8787. Monthly.
A magazine for single-lens reflex camera owners. Uses features on and illustrated by glamour photography. Also accepts photographs for picture files. Fees around £20 a published page.

What Camera Weekly

Haymarket Publishing Ltd, 38-42 Hampton Road, Teddington, Middlesex TW11 0JE; telephone 01-977 8787. Weekly.
The equipment bias of early issues of this magazine is less noticeable now. It requires

features on any photographic techniques, giving good scope for the use of glamour pictures. Features should normally run to around 1000 words, with about seven pictures. Fees are negotiable.

Newspapers and magazines

There are thousands of newspapers and magazines published in Britain. Many of them offer markets for glamour photographs.
Local newspapers will often run pictures of local girls to brighten their pages. Payment may be poor, or even non-existent, but a credit line for the photographer can be useful publicity.
National daily newspapers, such as *The Sun* and *Daily Star,* have a regular pin-up picture page.
Unlikely looking magazine titles can also offer markets. *Popular Motoring* has run a regular pin-up spot on its news pages. Originally, this featured a girl with a motoring connection (such as holding a greasy spanner!), but even this link was not always there.
If you are able to come up with a series of pictures linking glamour to a particular specialist interest, there is almost certain to be a magazine around that will be able to use it somewhere among the pages.
There is only one reliable way to search out these potential markets. Go to the largest newsagent in your area and thumb through all the publications one by one. Buy a copy of anything which appears to offer potential.
It is also useful to have a directory of magazines and newspapers for reference. Apart from anything else, no newsagent can stock every publication, so a directory will help you find some of those which are worth buying direct from the publishers.

There are two useful directories for the freelance photographer.

Writers' & Artists' Yearbook.

Published annually by A. & C. Black (Publishers) Ltd, 35 Bedford Row, London WC1R 4JH; 1981 edition £2.95. This inexpensive paperback should be on the bookshelves of every freelance photographer. It is by no means comprehensive (only *Mayfair, Men Only* and *Penthouse* in the men's magazine section, for example), but it lists requirements and fees, as well as addresses and telephone numbers. Also included is much other useful information for anyone involved in publishing and journalism.

British Rate & Data, 76

Oxford Street, London W1N 0HH. Published monthly; single copy £42. This mammoth publication contains advertising rates for all except the smallest UK newspapers and magazines. It is bought by advertising agencies and publishers, who normally take out the £90 annual subscription. From the freelance photographers' viewpoint, it is useful only for the comprehensive list of titles and addresses it provides. Titles are indexed both alphabetically and by classification. Advertising rates change frequently, which is why *'Brad'* appears monthly. Changes of titles and addresses are less frequent, so one copy every year or so would suit most freelance contributors. Expensive, but very useful. However, since *'Brad'* is published monthly, most advertising agencies and publishers are throwing away very recent issues. If you have a good contact with an agency or publisher, you might be able to obtain this 'out-of-date' copy for nothing.

Calendar publishers

Calendar publishing does not offer a very large market to the speculative glamour contributor. Many glamour shots for calendars are commissioned from well-known photographers. Other calendar publishers go to colour libraries for their material.

However, it does no harm to write to calendar publishers asking for details of their requirements. Build up your own contact list by noting the name and address of the publisher from any glamour calendar you come across. Here are two to start you off.

DRG Calendars & Diaries

Ltd, Hope Road, Bristol BS3 3NZ; telephone 0272 294294. Buys mainly 5 x 4in transparencies, but will consider smaller formats for glamour calendars. Fees from £30 to £80.

Lowe Aston Calendars Ltd,

Saltash, Cornwall PL12 4HL; telephone 075-55 2233. 5 x 4in transparencies only. Fees by negotiation.

Picture libraries

Terms and conditions for picture libraries and agencies vary quite widely. Always write for details of requirements before submitting any work. All the following libraries handle glamour photographs.

Fotolink Picture Library,

Lynwood House, 24/32 Kilburn High Road, London NW6 5XW; telephone 01-328 9221.
The Northern Picture

Library, Unit 2, Bentick Street Industrial Estate, Ellesmere Street, Manchester M15 4LN; telephone 061-236 4049.
PFB Photo-Library, 11 Hyde Park Crescent, Leeds LS6 2NW; telephone 0532

789869/742054.
Photo Library International,

St. Michaels Hall, Bennett Road, Leeds LS6 3HN; telephone 0532 789321.
Pictorial Press Ltd,

30 Aylesbury Street, London EC1R 0BL; telephone 01-253 4023.
Pictor International Ltd,

Lynwood House, 24/32 Kilburn High Road, London NW6 5XW; telephone 01-328 9221.
Rex Features Ltd, 18 Vine Hill,

London EC1R 5DX; telephone 01-278 7294.
Spectrum Colour Library,

146 Oxford Street, London W1; telephone 01-637 3682.
Stockphotos International,

131 High Holborn, London WC1; telephone 01-405 4668.

Models and model agencies

There are several ways you can obtain a model for glamour photography.

First, there is the direct approach, asking a girl you see in a shop or office, meet in a pub, or pass in the street. Even if you get a good rate of acceptance, you will find that not all girls who look good will photograph as well. However, you may not need to pay very high fees initially. Also, you will have a girl who has not been used before by glamour publications.

Second, you can place an advertisement for models in the window of a local shop, in a local newspaper, or in one of the national photographic magazines. This will not cost very much, but you will be lucky if one in ten of the girls replying are suitable. Only one in a hundred will prove to be the perfect glamour model.

Third, you can reply to model advertisements which appear in the photographic magazines. This is almost as unreliable as placing your own advertisement, since most of the girls featured in the classified sections are not suitable for quality glamour photography. However, there are exceptions, so it does no harm to write off to the box numbers given. Do not part with more than about 50p for a photograph.

Fourth, you can make use of a studio which supplies models. Here, you should be able to choose from a selection of photographs. If the studio is for amateur photographers, the model fees are likely to be quite low. This means that the studio will not attract top models. However, you could find a girl who is just starting modelling and has good potential.

Fifth, you can go to a professional model agency. This is usually the best way to book a model, since most of the girls on the books will have had training and experience. Although more expensive than the other methods, booking an agency model usually means that you will be able to shoot a lot of saleable pictures in a short photo session.

Not all agencies will deal with inexperienced photographers. The girls on their books will be wary of posing for people who produce inferior pictures. Before you make contact with these agencies, put together a good portfolio of your best photographs, showing that you have a professional approach to the subject. It will also help if you have a scrapbook of published work.

Arrange to call at the agency, so that they have a chance to meet you, and so that you can discuss your requirements. Be very aware that they will be reluctant to send a girl to your home studio unless you can offer good references.

Local model agencies can be found in British Telecom Yellow Pages under 'Model Agencies.'

Here is a list of some of the better-known model agencies.

London

Geoff Wootten, 52 Brittania Road, Fulham, London SW6; telephone 01-763 0191.

International Model Agency, 2 Hindle Street, London W1; telephone 01-486 3312.

Samantha Bond Management, 241 Kings Road, London SW3 5UA; telephone 01-352 3767.

Sarah Cape Model Agency, Folly Mews, 223a Portobello Road, London W11; telephone 01-229 2068.

Top Models, 37 Percy Street, London W1; telephone 01-636 8771.

Top Team International, 143 New Bond Street, London W1; telephone 01-491 3872.

Yvonne Paul Management Ltd, 35 Kempe Street, London NW6; telephone 01-960 0022.

Outside London

Bridget Atkinson Model Agency, 6 King Street, Blackpool, Lancashire; telephone 0253 22019.

Birmingham Model Agency, Gloucester House, Smallbrook, Queensway, Birmingham B5 4HP; telephone 021-643 1547.

Bluebell Model Agency International, Suite 2, 1-3 Haywra Crescent, East Parade, Harrogate, North Yorkshire HG1 3BG; telephone 0423 504767.

Patricia Brooks Model Agency, 56 Lister Grove, Heysham Lancashire LA3 2DG; telephone 0524 51403.

Charmers Index, 20 Colegate, Norwich, Norfolk NR3 1BQ; telephone 0603 613834.

Lucie Clayton, 30A King Street, Manchester; telephone 061-834 7471.

Davis Hamilton, 166 Buchanan Street, Glasgow G1 2LW; telephone 041-332 3951/1915.

Louise Dyson Agency, 12 Frederick Road, Edgbaston, Birmingham B15 1JD; telephone 021-454 8614/5.

Elle Model Agency, 17 Hamilton Square, Birkenhead, Merseyside; telephone 051-647 4836.

Faces, 4 Rodney Street, Liverpool L1 2TE; telephone 051-709 5859.

The Pamela Holt Model Agency, 31 King Street West, Manchester M3 2PF; telephone 061-834 6741.

Jaclyn Model Agency, Thackery House, Hempnall, Norwich NR15 2LP; telephone 050842 241.

Pat Keeling Model Agency, 99-101 Highcross Street, Leicester; telephone 0533 22540.

Jennie Lowe Model Agency, 75a Bold Street, Liverpool L1 4EZ; telephone 051-709 3515.

Manchester Model Agency, 57-63 Princess Street, Manchester M2 4EQ; telephone 061-236 1335/6.

The Julia Rose Agency, Pickwick House, 8 Needless Alley, New Street, Birmingham B2 5AE; telephone 021-632 5894/5.

Sally Stewart Model Agency Ltd, 2nd Floor, 74 Pembroke Road, Clifton, Bristol BS8 3EG; telephone 0272 30930/33055.

Supergirls, 18 Station Road, Solihull, West Midlands; telephone 021-704 3225/6/7.

Charlotte West Model Agency, 8a Cotham Hill, Bristol BS6 6LF; telephone 0272 314321.

Sue Williamson Agency, 15 Greenfield Crescent, Birmingham B15 3AU; telephone 021-454 3667/8.

Studios

None of the six photographers featured in this book uses a purpose-designed photographic studio. All take their indoor glamour pictures in a room of their own house or flat.

An area ten feet square is just adequate for glamour photography, so most photographers should be able to find somewhere to shoot at home.

The advantages of a home studio include the lack of a time limit and easy access to household props and accessories.

Adequate lighting equipment can be bought from around £100 – a cost which will soon be recouped in studio hire savings.

However, there may be times when you need the lighting or space which can be offered by some of the better studios. Here is a directory of some of them. Write for full details of the facilities available. Fees are from £5 an hour.

Beehive Centre of Photography,
136 Gloucester Avenue, London NW1; telephone 01-586 4916.
Leeds Model Agency,
11a Hyde Park Crescent, Leeds LS6 2NW; telephone 0532 789869/742054.
Talbot Photographics,
Alwych House, Bethel Street, Norwich NR2 1NR; telephone 0603 29052.
Unit 15, Springfield Industrial Estate, Farsley, Pudsey, West Yorkshire; telephone 0532 572050.
Willow Photographic,
45 Bridge Street, Godalming, Surrey; telephone 048 68 5441/2.

Many photographic studios also advertise regularly in photographic magazines.

Processing laboratories

A good processing laboratory offering a personal service is essential to any freelance photographer.

Unfortunately, much 35mm transparency glamour work must be shot on Kodachrome film. This excellent material has to be returned to Kodak, where it is processed to the highest standards – but the service lacks any personal touch. You usually have to rely on the post to send and return your film – which can sometimes be in the Kodak laboratories for over a week during the peak processing season.

Ektachrome film users are better served. Most independent laboratories offer the necessary E6 processing. If a laboratory is near enough, you may be able to take advantage of a same day service, since the process itself only takes a couple of hours from start to finish.

You can find details of local laboratories in British Telecom Yellow Pages under 'Photographic Processors and Finishers.'

If there is no laboratory near enough for you to visit, you can choose from the many which advertise in the pages of photographic magazines. However, you must expect to lose the occasional film in the post. If a film contains shots which have cost you a lot of money – an overseas assignment, for example – it is well worth using registered post. Tell the laboratory that the film is special, too.

It is not worth home-processing your colour film. The savings in cost will be off-set by the time it takes. Also, you will not be able to produce consistent results without spending a lot of money on temperature control equipment.

Presentation packs

Some magazine contributors send their black-and-white prints interleaved with pieces of paper. They also wrap each glass-mounted slide in tissue paper before sealing them up with large amounts of sticky tape, string and wrapping paper!

This is not the way to put any editor or picture buyer in a good mood. Picture editors are unpacking and repacking photographs all the time. If your pictures slide out of the envelope and are easy to look at, you start off on the right foot. Good presentation material is not cheap. It is often more expensive than the material cost of the pictures. But it protects your potentially-valuable work, and it makes life a lot easier for everyone you deal with.

Prints simply require a stiff card envelope. Second-best is an ordinary large envelope with two sheets of card inserted to prevent it being folded. This is much more effective than a 'Do not bend' label.

Slides can be presented in a number of ways. Most effective are black card masks. These measure around 5 x 4in and have a central aperture cut for the format of film you require. The bright colours of your slides contrast well against the card.

Avoid using the larger sheets of card which have several apertures and will hold six or more transparencies. Picture editors like to sort photographs into 'hold' and 'reject' piles, so they need slides presented individually.

If your slides have been mounted by the processing laboratory, you can use plastic sheets with pockets. These sheets will hold a dozen or more mounts quite securely, protecting them from dust and fingerprints.

Slides do not need mounting for projection. Few picture editors ever use a projector. The initial selection is made with the naked eye, followed by an inspection by high-power magnifier of the chosen transparencies. Never post glass mounts.

Remember to check that the return packing you enclose with your submissions is actually large enough to take the slides and their presentation material!
Here are some of the companies which supply presentation packs. Brochures and price lists are available on request.

DW Viewpacks Ltd, Unit 2, Peverel Drive, Granby, Bletchley, Milton Keynes MK1 1NL; telephone 0908 642323/642373. Plastic sheets for slide storage and presentation, plus slide library systems.

Javerette Ltd, 83 Duke Street, Grosvenor Square, London W1M 5DJ; telephone 01-629 2756/0788. Black card masks and transparency sleeves.

Kenro Photographic Products, High Street, Kempsford, near Cirencester, Gloucestershire GL7 4EQ; telephone 028 581 426/7. Black cards masks, plastic sheets for slide storage, library systems, and other presentation materials.

Eric Fishwick Ltd, Grange Valley, Haydock, St. Helens, Merseyside WA11 0XE; telephone 0744 27384/5/6. Postal cartons, printed 'Photographs, Do Not Bend.'

Studio flash

Studio electronic flash is ideal for most glamour photography. Full details about some of the different systems are available from the following manufacturers and distributors.

Bowens of London, Royalty House, 72 Dean Street, London W1V 6DQ; telephone 01-439 1781. Bowens flash systems.

Courtenay Photonics, Photonics House, Horsham Road, Dorking, Surrey RH4 2JN; telephone 0306 3720. Courtenay flash systems.

Jessop of Leicester Ltd, Photo Centre, Hinckley Road, Leicester LE3 0TE; telephone 0533 20461. Powerflash flash systems.

Keith Johnson Photographic, 1/2 Ramillies House, Ramillies Street, London W1V 1DF. Multiblitz flash systems.

Studio accessories

Studio Accessories, 443/449 Waterloo Road, Blackpool, Lancashire; telephone 0253 694340. Painted backgrounds, posing props and a wide range of accessories.

Wiggins Teape Paper Ltd, Gateway House, Basing View, Basingstoke, Hampshire RG21 3NZ; telephone 0256 20262. Colorama background paper.

Useful organisations

Association of Fashion, Advertising and Editorial Photographers,
10a Dryden Street, Covent Garden, London WC2; telephone 01-240 1171.

Association of Photographic Laboratories, 50 Great Russell Street, London WC1; telephone 01-405 2762.

British Association of Picture Libraries and Agencies,
27 Orchard Way, Bubbenhall, Warwickshire; telephone 0203 306348.

Bureau of Freelance Photographers, Focus House, 497 Green Lanes, London N13 4BP; telephone 01-882 3315/6.

The BFP has a worldwide membership of around 12,000 – not only full-time freelances, but also amateur and semi-professional photographers. It is primarily a service organisation, with membership open to anyone with an interest in freelance photography.
The most useful service provided by the Bureau is the

Market Newsletter. Widely regarded as the most authoritative publication of its kind, this well-researched monthly letter keeps members in touch with the market for freelance pictures. It gives full information about the type of pictures currently being sought by a wide range of publications and other outlets, and predicts trends and development in the market. Other services provided for a modest annual subscription including *Market Survey Specials,* covering glamour and calendar markets, among others; free advice on all aspects of freelancing, including the use of agencies; recovery of unpaid reproduction fees; and specially-designed submission and model release forms.

Institute of Incorporated Photographers, Amwell End, Ware, Hertfordshire; telephone 0920 4011/2.

Institute of Journalists, Bedford Chambers, Covent Garden, London WC2E 8HA; telephone 01-836 6541.

Irish Professional Photographers Association, 12 Ludford Street, Dublin 14, Ireland.

Master Photographers Association, 1 West Ruislip Station, Ruislip, Middlesex HA4 7DW; telephone 089 56 34515.

National Union of Journalists, Acorn House, 314 Gray's Inn Road, London WC1; telephone 01-278 7916.

Photographic Dealers Association, Photographic House, 84 Newman Street, London W1P 3LD; telephone 01-323 4641.

Professional Photographers Association of Northern Ireland, 16 Mill Street, Comber, Newtonards, Co. Down, Northern Ireland.

The Royal Photographic Society, The Octagon, Milsom Street, Bath BA1 1DN; telephone 0225 62841.